# The Corporate Prophet
## A fresh take on management, integrated and simplified

Mohan Pandey

This is a work of fiction. Characters and situations are created for instructional purposes only. Any resemblance with any real person, organization or situation is purely coincidental.

Mohan Pandey asserts his moral right to be recognized as the author of this work.

Author website: www.mohanpandey.in
Cover Concept: Smita, www.trulearn.com
Cover Photo: James Thew, www.fotolia.com
Primary Editing: Debasree, www.pothi.com

Copyright © 2012 Mohan Pandey
All rights reserved.

ISBN: 1-4750-8686-5
ISBN-13: 9781475086867

All rights reserved. No part of this work may be reproduced, stored or transmitted, in any form or by any means whatsoever (including but not limited to electronic, mechanical, and paper), without the prior written permission of the author.

*For those noble souls in the world of business*

*who have dedicated themselves to the pursuit of*

*the Truth, the Good and the Beauty.*

## *Contents*

| | |
|---|---|
| 1. Morning: The Meeting | 3 |
| 2. Organization | 11 |
| 3. Purpose | 15 |
| 4. Vision | 19 |
| 5. Strategy | 23 |
| 6. Systems Thinking | 27 |
| 7. Decision Making | 33 |
| 8. Value | 37 |
| 9. Finance | 43 |
| 10. Innovation | 51 |
| 11. Risk and Uncertainty | 59 |
| 12. Marketing and Sales | 63 |
| 13. People | 69 |
| 14. Managing Self | 75 |
| 15. Managing Others | 83 |
| 16. Learning | 93 |
| 17. Production and Delivery | 101 |
| 18. Execution | 107 |
| 19. Change | 113 |
| 20. Sustainability | 117 |
| 21. Society | 121 |

| | |
|---|---|
| 22. Ethics | 125 |
| 23. Leadership | 129 |
| 24. Evening: The Dinner | 133 |

*Look within (chapters)*

*In this world (2-6),
decide how you would be useful (7-12),
set up what you need to be useful (13-16),
deliver what you promise (17-18),
sustain (19-20)
and leave a legacy (21-23).*

# May you find your own path!

As far back as recorded human history goes, we find evidence of our yearning for true meaning. Repeatedly, we are urged to search for that meaning within us. We are guided by the powerful aphorisms like 'know thyself' in the Occident to 'thou art that' in the Orient. Such timeless truth is shared for the common good in a beautiful manner.

Unfortunately, it is difficult, if not impossible, to find such guidance in the world of business. 'Business of business is business' doesn't quite rank up there. And that despite the fact, that there are hundreds of excellent books written by researchers and by practitioners. In the past five or six decades, we have witnessed a tremendous amount of knowledge generation. We did witness waves of fads and fashion, but we do also have some profound wisdom. That is indeed of immense value. Nevertheless, some gaps remain.

One key dimension is the need to explore the integration of the various specialties and super-specialties. Further, there is the need to recognize that businesses do not exist in a vacuum. We as human beings live in a complex world. We form businesses that in turn live in the same complex world. I would not be charged with exaggeration if I used the phrase 'chaotic and complex world', instead of 'complex world'. If that was not enough, the rate of change and the scale of scope in our times are unprecedented for humanity.

I have no fight with super-specialization. All I am trying to advocate is that we need to develop an appreciation for the big picture. That appreciation must also help us as we grapple with some fundamental issues of our era. How do we—as individuals, families, societies and nations—fit in this world and how do we fit as an employee, as a professional and as an entrepreneur? How do we affect our environment while the environment affects us? Why are we not becoming happier as we are becoming prosperous? Why are we getting depressed every now and then, when we thought we had everything worked out? Why do we have work-life issues all around us? Where did we lose our spirit behind?

While these questions are of extreme importance to us, I contend that this is not for the first time that humanity is faced with such questions. Corporations as we know today are a new form of social order, and therefore the questions look new to us. But I believe, throughout the course of history and in societies all over the world, people have attempted to deal with these.

There is, I believe, much to be learnt when we embark on our journey of finding new answers.

While there are, for sure, many ways we could look at the subject, what I have found particularly enlightening and useful is the concept of this fascinating triad—The Truth, The Good, and The Beauty. It was quite a revelation to me to find that this, in many variants, has emerged in both Occidental and Oriental traditions. That's the guiding principle I have adopted.

This book is a humble attempt to bring an integrated picture and synthesize some key insights for the benefit of the readers. This is a single story, which is presented in chapters simply for convenience.

Early scribbling from my management school days kept evolving as I grew in my corporate roles. It took me ten years to complete this book. Guess what, it feels like the beginning of a quest. I'm excited about the journey that begins now.

I felt comfortable using the 'dialogue' model in line with the Oriental traditions of discourse and am specifically indebted to Khalil Gibran's celebrated book 'The Prophet' in creating the plot. While you would notice a story line here, this is not a novel. The plot is there to enable the ideas forwarded. I wish I were a better storyteller.

Nevertheless, I hope it's an easy read, which would offer you several 'aha' moments. It was indeed a great challenge to keep the book to a small size. Many a times during the last ten years, it grew oversize and I had to burn the midnight oil to condense it. On other occasions, I felt like offering just the code, and letting the reader figure the puzzle out. I hope I managed to strike a balance. I trust it would catalyze your own thinking and motivate you to learn more.

May you find your own path!

My parents Parbati and Chandrama Pandey and my elder sister Sarandha made me what I am. My friends, my teachers and my mentors shaped my worldview. Of course, so did the countless masters whose books I read. Where do I start acknowledging and where do I stop?

Very early feedback on the concept from Deepti Jerath and Sunil Handa set me on the right path. I benefitted a lot from the encouragement and advice I received from the early reviewers of the manuscript—Scott Grossman, Balu Balasubramanian, Marie Leithauser, Vishwanath Poosala, Suresh Kankanwadi, Suresh Poosala, Ranjani Nellore, Divya Dube, and Srivatsan Krishnan. My current employers were supportive all this while and I am grateful to them for that.

While I started writing with an intention to structure my thoughts for myself, I got motivated to complete this book because of my lovely sons Abhyuday and Nishreyas—this is my gift to them, my legacy.

As much as I was motivated, I would not have been able to succeed in this endeavor if I did not have the blessing of love and care of Smita, my wife. It would not be a hyperbole to say that this book is our co-creation.

While the credit of the success of this book goes to many, shortcomings are solely due to me.

Mohan Pandey
Bangalore
Feb 29, 2012

# The Corporate Prophet

# 1. Morning: The Meeting

As usual, Kris M, Chief Executive Officer of the Revered Enterprises Inc., parked his small electric car in the farthest parking lot. As he prepared to get out of the car, he noticed his mismatched socks and murmured to himself, "what a coincidence!" He promptly put that moment aside and grabbed his laptop bag, deliberately avoiding dwelling on the shining golden 'K' that looked so elegant against the black leather. He walked those two hundred yards slowly, as if he was accounting for each of the fallen leaves on the pathway, stopping a couple of times to take a few deep breaths. He wished 'Good Morning' as he walked past Mrs. Perez who was cleaning the carpet in the corridor that led to his office. She wished him back—a tinge of surprise in her eyes. He simply was too early today. A living legend, he had been with this large multinational corporation for a decade and half and had risen through the ranks to become the CEO.

Last night, after pondering over the recent developments for several weeks, he had concluded that it was time to move on. The latest piece of information was too strong to ignore. He remembered his conversation

Mohan Pandey

with Maya, his wife, after dinner last night. She had hugged him tight and said, 'I'm with you', and then told him that he had no need to lose sleep over this matter. Before going to bed, he had put a meeting on the calendar of his senior leadership team and had logged off to sleep.

He looked at his watch; still an hour to go, and gazed out, yet again, beyond the clear window—out to the Atlantic. He opened the window and a gush of breeze came from the east, and filled his heart with joy, as much as with yearning.

Then as he looked, exactly nowhere, he felt restless, and thought:

"Fifteen years ago, when I joined this company as a trainee, I witnessed one fifth of the staff getting retrenched within a matter of months. Financials were in such a bad shape—so many rounds of layoffs. It could be anybody's turn, anytime. It's been a long journey from there to what it is today—the most sustainable enterprise in the world. A company loved by its employees, customers, investors and society at large. All that I had, I gave to the organization and to no one else, in thoughts, in speech and in action. Fifteen years! As I leave, it seems, I'm offering to leave my body. And what I'm leaving behind, it seems, is nothing else but my mind and my heart. Yet, it's time now that I cannot hold myself any longer."

## The Corporate Prophet

"Now, whatever time is left for me should be devoted to this special calling. I've made my decision. I have to count my blessings too and not just hold on to the thoughts of pain and suffering."

"Even if I could split myself into two, won't I wish to be split again? I am but one."

He looked again at his watch, and was amused at the thought that Time did not slow down to admire that beautiful piece of art—a special gift on their tenth wedding anniversary from Maya. Ages! Yet, no longer than a while.

"Oh, I got to take some rest," he thought, and took his morning pill before settling down in the couch. "Thank you my companion, you're making this journey bearable," he said as he admired that little bottle of pills.

As he sat down, he looked at the artwork at his desk. Seven stars, arranged as in Ursa Major with a smiling face in each of them. "These six friends who steered this company to further and further growth, are coming to see me, rather, whom I want to see, won't they be shocked to find me putting down my papers suddenly?"

"For they have loved me so much, and I have also loved them all. Those heated discussions and warm evenings, common breakfasts and small celebrations made us a beautiful family, really close-knit. Ever since they joined, none of them left this small beautiful group. And they all in turn, in their functions, have replicated the same, and thus it's now an organization of nine thousand three hundred and thirty one."

"Oh, this day of parting will be a day of togetherness, and will not they all urge me to stay back? And, what would I say to them? And, will it be so that I would have a new start this day?"

"Maya believes I've something special in me. Maybe it's just her love speaking. She wants me to pass on my wisdom to my team. She also wants me to put my thoughts in a book. I've never done anything like that...."

"If this is that day of parting, can I take a fresh look of whatever I did? Will I be able to think straight? Oh, why does a day of parting ever come? Oh, the ways of heart unknown!"

"And would it be possible to take a fresh look on all the systems developed, processes defined and knowledge created over a fifteen long years, which had so many days and so many nights."

He moved to the hall, which was lovingly called 'The Knowledge Room'. He found none of the six was missing, and heard a unified voice greeting him—'Hi Kris!' They were always very close and well aligned.

# The Corporate Prophet

"Hi friends!" he waved back and took his chair, as he always did, and in a great voice full of power, and love, and concern, he started to speak, "My friends, you all know me very well and you know that you own me as much as my family does or as much as my country does. And only because of that you'll be able to see, what I see".

"I'm deeply moved by the problems children across the world are facing these days. I recently had an opportunity to visit several pediatric hospitals, orphanages and schools. I want to do whatever little I can to change the situation. I've been thinking about it for some time, and I guess the time for action is now."

He paused to assess the reaction—six faces and twelve eyes—and saw a silent stillness as if they were images and not living beings. He started again:

"I've decided to resign. I'm going to make an effort with whatever I have and help the kids. Thus, with a heavy heart and deep sorrow, I'm putting down my papers and preparing to leave. Yes, difficult as it indeed is."

They were all looking at each other and then at him, their boss, nay, their Kris. And they all said, "Please, don't go," and added "take a long leave, if you have to, and then come back. All of us are ready to contribute, whatever we can to the cause". He was overwhelmed with emotions, but then, was that unexpected?

"I know how much you all love me, and would like to help me. However, my friends, this is something I have to do personally, and—immediately."

"And, in fact, you shouldn't try to stop me from going, for you love me. For you love me you know, I'll be yours wherever I am. And think if it were death taking me away, would you get a chance to plead your case?"

They were all crying in their hearts, but kept their tears inside. And Kathleen said:

"It all seemed so natural, this phenomenal growth. But don't you think we will not be able to maintain it from now on? Of course, we never thought we would ever need to ask such a question."

"Deep is your desire to follow your calling, and our love wouldn't stop you nor would our needs."

"Yet, this we do ask before you leave us, give us the essence, the essence of leading a great enterprise."

"And we will pass it on to our teams and they in turn will pass it to theirs, and that essence shall never perish."

"You have observed us work and have organized what we do, and you alone with a unique genius have seen how the causality unfolds. Now therefore disclose it to us, and tell us what brings success?"

## The Corporate Prophet

Kathy had a knack for numbers and knotty problems. She could solve the Rubik's cube when she was just five or six. She was quite comfortable running a lending and borrowing operation even when she was in high school. She worked with a top investment bank for about ten years before joining this organization a couple of years ago after the sudden unexpected demise of Soto, the previous CFO. She was admired for her straightforward and fearless attitude of questioning real hard—everything and everyone, including herself.

Kris, who was listening intently all along, said, "Kathy, as you know, we have a defined and deep succession plan in place. One of the key jobs of a leader is to groom the future leaders. Trust me, with the kind of team we have, we would move from success to success. Nevertheless, before we can know how to attain success, we need to know the definition of success. And at the same time, understand both the subject and the object of success."

"Of course", commented Ondatje, "as we have always believed, it's the organization's success that we want, and by success we mean achieving our targets".

Ony, the Head of Marketing, had earned his stripes in marketing in the interiors of Africa, where he pioneered the concept of daily use packs for almost all grocery items thus making them affordable to the poor. When somebody told him of the 'Bottom of the

Mohan Pandey

Pyramid' concept, he is said to have commented, 'we do have pyramids in Africa." His campaign, 'We Never Discount You', for a retail chain was considered one of the most innovative campaigns ever, and a case study must for all students of marketing.

"So'" said Kris, "let us understand first what an organization is".

## 2. Organization

"Organizations are vehicle of value creation, capture and delivery. They would have, within themselves, different organs that with functions like interaction with the environment, assembly of resources, use of resources to create value, means to capture the value thus created and mechanisms to deliver this value back to the environment. They are more than sum of parts, not just in quantitative sense, but also qualitatively because they have many properties that the parts cannot have."

"Even then, an organization is but a transient being. It is born; it grows, matures, ages and ultimately dies. As for all forms of life, these phases are inevitable for an organization too. Of course, there are differences in the life span, speed of growth, and levels of maturity reached, but all organizations, would eventually, follow this same pattern. Surely, the organizations that learn the virtue of remaining lean and healthy can increase their life span. But they must realize that they all must die."

He could see his colleagues turning white. He continued thus:

Mohan Pandey

"Death is, however, a mere change of form. As the ice melts with an increase in temperature, it starts dying. When it has melted completely, it's dead. So to say, but, in fact, it only changed its form."

"Wait a moment, Kris", said Kathleen, "I'm getting somewhat confused. On one hand you're saying that death is inevitable, on the other, you're saying nothing dies..." she shrugged.

Kris nodded to express that he understood the confusion, and said, "life is eternal, living beings are not."

"Similarly", he continued, "the wheel of the economy keeps rolling, though industries transform and companies collapse. However, the end of a company only means that its constituents have come out of the oneness they hitherto belonged to, and have become one with other companies, other businesses."

"But then", said Kathleen, "Don't we know of companies which have survived for more than a century!"

"Yes", replied Kris, "indeed we know of companies which have lived for more than a century and of men and women who live to see more than a hundred springs in their lives. Indeed, we know of species as well, which live for three centuries or more. However, Kathy, that doesn't mean they are immortal."

"Agreed Kris, that impermanence is one of the attributes of an organization," said John, the COO and

Kris' best friend, "but what is an organization"?John was one of the brightest students of the University of Life. He was a self-made man who could afford to start schooling only when he was twelve—as he was already earning higher wages as a store assistant. He was offered that job because the store manager had recognized his knack of organizing merchandise in the most customer-friendly manner yet maximizing the space utilization. His 190 IQ ensured that it took him just three years to catch up with others—and then he moved faster than anybody else did by becoming one of the youngest graduates in operations research from one of the Ivy League institutes.

Kris, aware of the fact that John knew the answer but just wanted to ensure everyone got it right, smiled and replied:

"An organization is a structure and a system that functions. For example, a human body is an organization. It has cells, tissues, organs etc, providing the structure. At the same time, it has systems like, central nervous systems, cell-signaling systems etc. providing the processes. The causal relationship is established and structures and systems are interwoven to make the body functional."

"Primarily, an organization performs just one function: interaction with the environment. Again, like a human body, it receives signals from the environment, interprets it, analyses it and responds. Also, through this, it influences the environment to the extent it can."

"So, for an organization, you need to define the physical structures as well as the systems and the processes that make it work. Your organization should be able to read the changes that happen in the environment, assimilate this information and quickly take decisions. In some cases, the brain would have time to think through, in some cases you should let the organs respond. By no means would you be able to predefine the decisions, but for sure, you will be able to define the values that define decision-making. So, never forget to ensure that everyone in the system understands these values."

At this time, he looked at Henry, who was the CIO, a college dropout who became part of this organization because of an acquisition, and said, "To you, Henry, an organization is an integration of hardware and software that works."

"Yes, very much so, hardware and software with an architecture appropriate for the purpose", murmured Henry.

"Precisely so, Henry," replied Kris, "an organization is able to work because it has a purpose and is able to deliver because its architecture fits the purpose."

# 3. Purpose

"In a given environment, an organization exists to serve a purpose. As the environment changes, the purpose changes and the organization becomes irrelevant. Then, it has to transform. Going back to the example of the ice, the complete melting of the ice just means that it has served its purpose of existence in an environment of low temperature. When there was no sun, it kept its molecules close and calm. The challenge is to survive until the purpose is served. For, if it died before that, it would have had a wasted life. The challenge is to engrave 'purpose served' on the milestone, the milestone of death, where you would have your form changed."

As everyone was again getting disturbed at the mention of the certainty of death, Kris walked up to the corner of the room to fill his cup of coffee. He came back, stood holding the backrest of his chair with his right hand, and said, "Friends, once we know of the certainty of death, it becomes easier going about making our lives purposeful. Purpose: Something that's beyond the given requirements of our physical, social and economic existence."

Mohan Pandey

"A scientist feeds herself by selling her inventions, but mere food is not her purpose. The Truth is."

"An economist pays his rent by helping others juggle the tussle between their limited resources and unlimited wants, but mere shelter is not his purpose. The Good is."

"An artist keeps himself warm by selling his art, but mere clothing is not his purpose. The Beauty is."

"Like a scientist, an economist and an artist, an organization has to find a purpose, the purpose of its existence. But remember, and I will come back to this again, it needs to exist before it can serve a purpose."

"So how do you choose The Truth, The Good or The Beauty, and aren't there many other dimensions hanging around that you need to worry for", asked John?

"Well,' Kris thought for a moment, "you follow your heart. Pick your calling; and the good news is that you can find things worth pursuing that belong to the intersection of these three dimensions. I still remember, the way you first described your innovative store layout as 'just so beautiful' and then said it made so much economic sense, and then you followed through with your research to mathematically prove why it was so. I still remember your beautiful mathematical equation, so simple, so elegant and yet so powerful. That's Truth."

John almost blushed.

## The Corporate Prophet

"And, to the point about the other factors, I must contend there are many. However, the concept of this triad dates back to ancient philosophers. Some of them felt that these dimensions completely define The One and that if we could create a harmony of these three in our lives and our societies, we would be closest to the image of The One. These three are like primary colors; everything else can be defined as a certain mix of these three. You could pursue any of these three and have a purposeful life. But, by God, the power that you derive at the intersection just blows you off! Pursuit of something meaningful that leads to something elegant that is beneficial for society. How elegant is this thought itself—working at the intersection of Science, Commerce and Arts—how useful, and you bet, meaningful!"

"Kris, indeed that's a beautiful thought," interrupted Hu, head of HR, "but help me understand how can all the organs of a body have one goal? The purpose of the brain is different from that of the heart. The purpose of the hands is different from that of the legs. Besides, when we talk of a corporate organization, there are thousands of people working in various functions, various markets. So do they all have one purpose?"

Hu was as an expert in psychology with an interesting doctoral work that led to the popular book 'When Confucius met Maslow: Hidden dimensions of human behavior". Her lateral thinking was extremely valued by everybody in the organization. Her capacity to work hard was the subject of folklore in the company. You would still find, a sepia photograph of her father working in the paddy fields, prominently displayed in her office.

"Hu," replied Kris, "the organs have different functions geared towards the same purpose. Our legs walk us to the food, our hand takes it up. Our heart pumps blood; our brain derives nutrition from fresh blood. In the end, they all work towards the purpose of the survival of the body. R&D brings new products to marketing; marketing brings an understanding of the needs of the environment; in the end, they all work towards satisfying a particular need of the end-user."

"In fact, that's where you need to start from—the end-user. To add value to the end-user what is it that you need to do. You may say that each of the functions has its own objectives, but they need to be so aligned as to link to the end-user. All functions need to confer with each other to ensure that they are aligned. That's very important, though it takes considerable effort."

"Is there something," Hu asked, "that can enable this alignment process?"

"Sure," Kris replied, "it's there. Not only does it ensure alignment it also makes it very efficient. That powerful something is called 'Vision' ".

# 4. Vision

"Vision is being able to dream. To dream of a destination where lives your love—your goal. To have the confidence that you'll meet it someday, somehow. And to know that it's you who has been gifted with this blessing by the Almighty."

"It's not a lamp burning somewhere far; it's just the knowledge that there is a lamp burning somewhere far."

"It's beyond the obvious, composed of the subtle and yet within your reach."

"It's something that tells you your path is right, as well as it tells you your path is wrong when it is so."

"It says to all the members of the caravan that all the camels should move together, as all the men should, and that they should move in but one direction. Of course, the ablest person leads it, but the vision is not her or his alone, it's of the caravan."

"Of course, they're all great players of their instruments, but what will happen to the symphony if the players do not stop when they should, or they do not play when they should play. And again, the vision is not of the maestro only, it's of the orchestra as a whole."

Mohan Pandey

"However, I must say, as much as a dream a vision is, it must be grounded in reality. The higher you move, the more things you see, but you see them less clearly. Therefore, as you move up, you try to memorize how it was down there, but when you have moved up, things that are down certainly have changed."

"And what about vision then, it surely pushes you up, but it says keep coming to earth, for vision is not something fictional. Vision is born of imagination, but is not imaginary."

"You have to open your eyes to see, and close them to dream, but if you don't see things with open eyes, your dreams will be but empty."

"I get goose-bumps thinking about this," commented John, "I mean the fact that this stuff 'Vision' does exist, like consciousness exists. Just reflect for a second on the complexity of this world. Then, it's not static, it's not predictable. And at what scale are we handling things these days! And then a belief in 'Order out of Chaos'. A vision that penetrates through the fog and mist of ignorance, like a powerful third eye. It's almost mystical."

Ony looked at John admiringly and then turned to Kris: "How can so many individuals in an organization have the same dream?"

## The Corporate Prophet

On hearing this, he closed his eyes for a while, and said, "Could you all shut your eyes for a moment, please?"

They all did.

He said very softly, "Stop thinking."

After a few minutes of silence he asked, "Have you stopped thinking?" They said they could not. He asked, "Tell me what went through your minds?" All of them said, in different words, that they thought of how they could hold him.

He smiled. "This is how different people can dream about the same thing. And what is a leader worth, without the vision and ability to make it everyone else's vision?"

"So you should have the vision of the organization clearly and carefully drafted and shared across the organization. It should be short and simple so that everyone in the organization can remember it."

"Don't miss any opportunity to remind your stakeholders, both internal and external, of the vision that your organization has."

"I cannot agree more", said Ony, "however, we have to be able to convert the vision to reality; your camels have to move and your instruments have to be tuned. And even before we get there, is there some tool available that helps in creation of vision and is there some metric that would separate a great vision from a not-so-great vision?"

Ony was always like that. The brass and tacks guy. Kris loved his style. So did everyone else in the team. They couldn't stop smiling when he tried to hunch his back when he mentioned the word camel.

Kris smiled too.

"Ony is on the money. First, let me mention that there's no tool per se that I can offer for vision creation. However, awareness of history and being reasonably aware of what's happening in the world helps. As far as metric is concerned, it's just now occurring to me that a vision of any worth should set you on at least one of the paths of the Triad. If it gets you on the intersection of any two of the elements of the Triad, it is an order better. As you can guess, the one that's at the intersection of all the three is of the highest order."

"Then to the other question Ony asked, you need to transcript your vision to purpose and support the purpose with appropriate strategy; of course, you need to have your organizational structure fit in with the strategy. Then you need to have a strategic plan that should be executed effectively."

"Stratos and agos, glamorous, isn't it?" quipped Kathy.

# 5. Strategy

"Strategy is the connector of the vision and the reality. Strategy is about making choices. You may not have control on the options that exist, but you do have control on the selection of the option for action. Be careful, however, because many a times the options may be hidden as are colors hidden in the white, and many a times you may be able to combine the colors to make shades and tints that you like."

"Those of you who play chess..." Kris turned to Henry to acknowledge the fact that Henry was an accomplished chess player who could play blindfold—maybe, because he was born in the city of birth of Bobby Fischer!

Kris continued, "...would know that the position that you desire is the strategy, the smaller steps that you take are tactics, and each tactical step may require multiple moves."

"As soon as you take a position, let us say 'cost driven' versus 'feature driven'; or say 'niche class' versus 'mass product' and so on, you would be forced to make trade-offs. While the generic strategy can be copied by anybody, the ways you structure the trade-offs and link your activities, would create your own unique strategic structure that would then help you offer distinctive value to your end-user."

"Well, I didn't get the trade-off bit," said Kathy, "you already kind of mentioned trade-off in selecting the position. What was this 'another trade-off'?"

Kris responded, "That's in selecting your activities."

"There are many paths and their permutations would probably reach your destination, however, you cannot walk two roads at a time, and hence, you need to include an option and exclude many others. You also need to select how you'd travel. You could fly through the firmament, sail through the sea or ride the road. Even if you decide to be on the ground, you need to decide if you want to walk with shoes or without shoes; walk during the day or walk during the night or both. Be wise not to foreclose those roads that you don't have to, because there is some value in keeping options open, though you don't know the value upfront. Whatever way you decide, consider for sure that you need to have the right vehicle and enough fuel for your vehicle and enough food for yourself as you make the journey; and carefully think through if you want to go alone or with a partner."

# The Corporate Prophet

"Remember though, be watchful but don't be stressed. For the end of one road is the beginning of another and you would like to last many more journeys."

"You may dwell for a moment or two on what has been accomplished and rejoice in your achievements, but should ponder a lot on lessons learnt and focus on what remains to be achieved, for the milestone tells you the distance to go and not the distance you have travelled."

As the spell broke, he heard someone asked, "Can we recap what steps we need to take when we formulate a strategy?"

Then he heard John enumerating those steps.

"First you need to establish what you are making a strategy for. This should be in alignment with the organization's vision. Second, you need to assess where you are currently against that parameter or those parameters. That'll give you the gap between the current state and the desired state. Since the future is uncertain, you have to understand that alternative scenarios around the desired state might exist. Then you'd chart out all the possible ways of bridging the gap. Finally, you'd select an option that is feasible, which at the same time is efficient in terms of generating maximum value per unit of input invested while minimizing the associated risks. Once you decide your position, you'd think through the trade-offs and linkages of your activities to create your unique strategy. You have to ensure that you're able to execute this strategy. Also, you should be able to frame this in a clear crisp form for further communication."

By now, he was fully back in the real world.

"I hope," Kris was in, "no one is imagining that it's a linear process."

"It's not. You should iterate as necessary."

"Also, oftentimes our statements are based on assumptions. While you are following those steps, be sure to challenge your assumptions. As a team, you must have processes that minimize the ill effect of personal biases as well as the disastrous effect of groupthink. Do not use the phrase 'strategic decision' to hide your limitation of understanding of the subject. Explicitly recognize the limitations. Get as good data as you can. Analyze it as well as is possible."

"One thinking methodology," remarked John, "that I've found particularly powerful in strategy formulation is called 'Systems Thinking', and I think I haven't seen a better practitioner of this than Kris."

# 6. Systems Thinking

Kris acknowledged the compliments with his peculiar humble smile. He started after a pause.

"Analysis is a powerful approach. It helps to reduce things, situations or problems and the scales of time to chunks that our brain can handle. Analysis though is just the beginning of comprehension, a process that ends with Synthesis."

"What we try to understand by slicing into two or more sections, is but one whole. And even if the parts may not appear to be linked, they are. All objects that we observe—can observe—and all objects that are hidden are related, directly or indirectly. The Moon is related to the Earth. The Earth is related to the Sun. It's easy to deduce that the Moon is related to the Sun as well."

"What we try to decipher by blocking in phases, is but one continuum. A road is a road; it's your choice to put stones by foot or by furlong. Remember, this imaginary road of time is nothing but a proxy for the change. The Moon has a cycle and the Earth has a cycle, and we ask how many cycles has the Moon completed while the Earth has completed one. You could pick any scale of your choice depending on the context. What you need to realize though is the fact that 'Time' is not a separate beast that comes from somewhere and does things."

"The innate energy in the elements of the Universe puts them in motion. Since everything is in motion, change happens."

"However, the pace of motion is not the same for all objects. Since each object is unique in itself and in its linkages, the change that it causes is unique. Likewise, the change that is caused to it is unique."

"Even if we're unable to catch up with the flux, because of our inability or inattention, cause leads to effect. Immediately after, this effect becomes a cause for leading to another effect, and so on. As much as the pond is muddled by the soil, the soil gets sodden due to the pond. This relationship is nothing but reflexivity."

"Parts of this whole, with their linkages, with their interactions, with their dynamism and with the inherent reflexivity constitute the system."

"I understand this; the whole universe is one system. Or, if I may say so, a system of systems. In terms that are more mundane the global economy is a system. Industries within this economy are systems. Companies within any industry are systems. Functions or processes within a company are systems. This realization is good, but one would be in a terrible situation if one gets overwhelmed by the enormity of this realization. More often

## The Corporate Prophet

than not, you would not be able to develop the correct understanding of the system. Even when you win that lottery, whatever you do would not create any impact on the mega system. Would one be right in assuming that as a mere drop in this ocean, one should just sit tight and do nothing?" With this statement, John raised his hands signaling surrender.

Kris nodded. At that moment, everyone's attention moved towards Ony. Kris exclaimed, "Ony, it looks like you're up to something." Ony was leaning back on his chair with his palms covering his eyes. He didn't change his posture immediately. After a couple of seconds, he moved his hands, opened his eyes and sat up straight.

"Well, Kris, I was trying to visualize John's comment", said Ony, "it was like a moment of truth."

"In these few moments I travelled back to my childhood. Six of us living in a ninety square foot room—home, if you will. Food was rationed to once a day. Toilets were flushed only twice a day because of lack of water. Electricity was non-existent. School, which was two miles away, was still attractive because they served lunch free, God bless them. Drugs were easily available in the neighborhood and extremely attractive because they offered guns like gifts. Everyone in that part of town had given up. The system won't change. In that very system, one day, I woke up. My teacher told

Mohan Pandey

me I was the best student she had ever had and that I was destined for a much bigger role in life. Honest to God, I never ever complained about the stinking, sweaty, dark nights but focused on studies. One thing led to another, one scholarship, one internship and then one day came when I looked back I had been part of a change that created many job opportunities, crime reduced, standard of life improved. I was only a minor contributor, but that's not the point. The point is this; in a ten year period even that pathetic system changed, for the better."

"Indeed so," John told the group, "last summer, Ony took me to his place, and his teacher still maintained that he was her best student ever."

Kris was gleaming. He took pride in his team and that was evident.

"What does this understanding mean in practical terms?" continued Kris. "Ony used the term 'visualization'. That's very important. Once we know the purpose of our effort, let us say, changing the strategy for our innovation portfolio, we should be able to represent the current state pictorially. And King, we don't need to start with the Big Bang and go down to the molecular level all the time," he winked.

King headed R&D, and was probably destined to get a Nobel, or two. He came from Scotland and was a great orator, with his presentations interspersed with

## The Corporate Prophet

typical British humor. He was known for his inclination towards explaining everything right from the first principles.

"The very first step is to identify the components. The second step is to link them. The third step is to mark the links to show if 'A' increases 'B' or if 'A' decreases 'B'. Close the loops. Remove the redundancies. Build a model and simulate the system, if you feel that's necessary. Now, you would be able to change the parameters and see how one thing affects another and the system as a whole. Get a hang of how a particular change, in this case, in portfolio strategy, impacts the end users, our employees or our finances. Let us say, due to pressure on the bottom-line we agree to cut the innovation portfolio. It would be obvious that we are cutting the future products off. So we probably were thinking of buying out some assets in future to fill the pipeline, once the business improved. Unfortunately, everyone else, by application of similar logic, would have exited innovation and there would be an industry wide dip. A long period of missed opportunity would ensue because building innovation capabilities take time. Once you get thinking on this line, it may occur that you may good deals in market for assets when everyone is exiting. You may then come around, take a contrarian stand, and position yourself strongly for the future uptick. Let me give a simpler example as well. If you cut on preventive maintenance, you would pay up by way of increased breakdown. Indirect costs of breakdown then may be significantly more than the direct savings generated through reduced maintenance. This is systems thinking, and that would help you enormously in decision making."

"Remember", Henry jumped in, "you don't need computers all the time. Many a times, closing your eyes and visualizing the way Ony did, is perfectly alright."

"Moreover," King added, "since you have to make so many decisions every day, you may not have the luxury of time to do all this. The key thing, however, is that you take a call. All the analysis, and synthesis, is useless if you don't actually take a decision."

"In time," quipped Hu.

"How much time you invest in making up your mind may depend on the enormity of the problem at hand and possibly the magnitude and scope of the impact it's going to have. It took me a blink to decide whom I wanted to make my life partner. That indeed is what we do in many scenarios. However, in an organizational setting, it's important to have the decision making process defined so that our stakeholders have confidence in the system. It does appear to be complicated, so let's understand how we make decisions and how we should make decisions," Kris paused.

# 7. Decision Making

Ony commented, "Situations demand that you decide. In the end, it is one simple question, 'Do I want to do this?'"

"That's correct," Kris responded, "and the decision would depend on your weltanschauung, which is your comprehensive conception of the universe, your coordinates and your linkages, let us say, your worldview. It includes your own knowledge and experiences, your access to the knowledge and experiences of others, your idea of causality and your assumptions of the future state."

"At the risk of repetition, let me mention that, it's true that, in many cases, all of this happens in a flash and we are unable to understand the process of making decision. We can afford to not understand the process for a lot of things that we do routinely, or in a personal capacity. However, it's important to not only make decisions but also to communicate how decisions are made when you are in a position of responsibility, as in our company, when you are trustees of the shareholders' money and all stakeholders' confidence."

"So how should that process look like?" Hu asked.

Mohan Pandey

"Well, why don't I recollect what Kris told me recently," John volunteered.

"First, you need to define the problem clearly—that could range from 'should we invest in this new technology' to 'should we move our offices to the suburbs' to 'should we hire one more person in production'. I mean, whether the scope is wide or narrow, the problem needs to be stated crisply."

"Then, make a good judgment of how much you want to invest in the process of decision making. You don't want to invest eight hours if the problem at hand is about one single cost item worth eight minutes of your time."

"Having done that, you need to define the criteria, which will help you assess both the benefits and the costs anticipated. For sure, list down all the explicit and implicit benefits and costs."

"You should also know the key stakeholders that need to be involved—those who can help you with the problem as well as those who will be impacted by your decision."

"Now you would have all the information that you need to help you make the decision. Based on the complexity and importance, use the information to generate values for the parameters that you have defined."

"Now, integrate this information logically. Decide. And, finally, communicate your decision to the key stakeholders with a brief on how the decision was made."

"Well said," Kathy jumped in, "and I'd like to add something."

"It's very important for everyone to know as to who is the Decision Maker. Many a times you'd find that decisions are pushed to committees and teams. That may be fine, but in those committees and teams, people should know if they are advisors, sole decision makers, or if they have a vote or a veto. What has worked well for us is the fact that we have individuals identified as decision makers who necessarily have an obligation to seek input from advisors and have a duty to communicate to all the key stakeholders. This makes the decision making process robust as well as rapid. And, definitely, for all key decisions, there are defined timelines. As Hu said once, 'late decision is no decision'."

"Amazing," Kris appreciated, "I don't think I would have said anything different on the subject. Let me ensure though that we don't miss an important dimension here."

"It's extremely important for the decision maker to be aware of his or her own biases and ensure that those biases do not compromise the quality of decision making. I may have a personal preference for a geography, King may have a personal preference for a technology, Kathy may have a personal preference for a financing model; such things should not cloud our decision-making. In all cases, and circumstances, we have to make decisions that maximize value for the company in a morally and legally positive way and in line with our commitment to sustainability. If we are not increasing value then probably we are eating away value created by others and we have no reason to be in business."

"Then I must ask what Value is?" King was forthright, as always.

# 8. Value

Kris responded to King, "When I say I value my family and my friends I'm making a subjective statement. When I say I value the work of Shakespeare or that of Mozart, again I'm making a subjective statement. Such subjective value proposition can, at best, be ranked on some arbitrary priority scale, but cannot really be quantified."

"On the other hand, an economic proposition would always have a quantifiable measure. That's universally true for anything, product or service, that's out in the market—that is, there is someone willing to sell and there is someone willing and capable of buying. For example, you cannot assign a value to the Statue of Liberty or to the Taj Mahal or to an act of bravery or to an act of charity; at the same time, you can always assign a value to items like a burger, a haircut, a movie show, a plane ride, a house, and so on."

"Economic value is a proxy for our expectations of future. Money is a means of quantifying economic value. You pay or commit to pay a certain amount of money expecting to get something in return."

Ony raised his hand as if in half salute, "when I talk about something as my value proposition to my customer, is that not as well some sort of economic value?"

Kris nodded, "indeed it is."

"This in fact is the central question to the existence of any commercial enterprise, 'Why would anybody pay you at all?', or simply put, 'What business are you in?' 'How do I convince my customer about the value he or she would derive?'"

"One clear case is when you are meeting an unmet need. Another is when you are offering a better solution on any or a combination of the following dimensions: Time, Space, Energy and Emotion. So, you got to make something faster, smaller, more energy efficient or appealing to any of the critical aspects of human psychology. The first three dimensions can be objectively universally defined, but the last one is subjective and population specific. Even if there is no other differentiation, making something more cost-effective itself can offer value. In all the cases, you should do a thorough research to understand your customer, and offer what the customer needs and not just what you think the customer needs."

"Just a sec," Kathy interjected after letting Kris finish his sentence, "didn't you say Shakespeare, Mozart, stuff that cannot be valued in terms of economics. So how does this Emotion dimension get in?"

"That's sharp," Kris looked at Kathy admiringly, "but you can pay real tangible money to buy an anthology or Shakespeare's plays or to buy a ticket to an opera. To sell these items, you appeal to the dimension of Emotion. Two timepieces may serve exactly the same function, but the better looking of the two may command a premium. While you are offering real value when you offer life insurance, to promote the same you may be appealing to emotion."

Kathy was still looking at Kris and thinking, "What emotional appeal would make you change your decision?" She quickly gathered herself to concentrate on what Kris was saying.

"I've always thought about business of business in very simple terms. Whatever my customer pays to buy my offering—whether product or service, my offering should make him more than that. Also, in the process, I should ensure that my company is rewarded enough by way of reasonable margins after accounting for all the direct and indirect costs including the cost of money. If I am consistent on this, I'd keep building value for my organization."

"Am I missing something," Hu said thoughtfully, "you didn't talk anything about the money we invest. Would that not decide the value to some extent?"

"What do you say," Kris replied with another question, "the value of your house is decided by the price you paid for it or by the price a buyer is willing to pay now?"

"Hmm," reflected Hu.

"What you have invested already is 'sunk cost'," pitched in Kathy, "that has no bearing at all on value. That investment is part of your system now. Value depends on what you do with that investment and not the investment itself." Kathy's eyes brightened.

"Makes sense," pondered Hu, "and cost of money is the interest I pay on my home loan."

"Or, the interest you forego if you invest your money in any company," Kathy was enjoying herself.

"Isn't this all too abstract?" asked John.

"Nope," smiled Kris, "it's all very tangible. Much like your wallet, and the green bucks that are in there."

"Well I hardly carry any cash these days", John joked.

"That's the point—money need not even be tangible, but it can be converted into tangible things. After all, even the green bucks are nothing else but a promise to pay. As long as that promise is good, money can take any form, paper, copper, or electronic data stored in your bank's server." Henry was on his home turf.

Kris continued. "Value is a singular number at the time of transaction, specific to the transaction, the buyer and the seller. At a different time, with a different buyer and with a different seller the value might change. And, that is because expectations of future held by different individuals are different, and they change fairly rapidly in this dynamic world."

He turned to Kathy, "this is really your expertise area, why don't you explain it further?"

"Sure," started Kathy, "you see that dynamism reflected in the stock market."

# 9. Finance

"Essentially you model the expected cash flows and adjust them back for the time value of money and the risk involved. The concept is not too difficult to grasp. But before that, let me mention that finance is like life-blood to the organizations. You like it or not, no business would run without finance. It also gives a very good way of tracking value creation—you would be increasing value if you increase income, decrease expense, increase sustainability and decrease uncertainty. That's something you can tell everybody in the organization. Anyone whose action is leading to any of these four outcomes, is doing good; provided that action is not affecting other dimensions to negate the good done on any one dimension."

"Going back to the concept, there are two aspects that you need to consider."

"For the first part, a dollar today is worth more than a dollar tomorrow. We are tuned to this idea since the agrarian revolution perhaps. If I give you an acre of land, and you return that after one year, I'd like to factor in the value of the crops. If I give you a pair of sheep, and you return that after one year, I'd like to factor in the value of milk, the wool and may be the litter as well."

"For the second part, we've all heard the saying a bird in hand is worth two in the bush. Similarly, a dollar in hand is worth more than a fifty-fifty chance of earning two dollars. So, if I ask you to part with your money and thereby introduce uncertainty for you, you'd ask to be compensated for the risk."

"Such adjustments are done through what we call 'discounting'. The farther in future the cash flow, higher the discounting. Greater the risk to the cash flow, higher the discounting."

"Now the output of this calculation would be as good as your estimates of the cash flow and discount rates. So, you need to carefully project the income and expenses out in the future. Also, you need to use the correct discount rates."

"Wait a minute", Ony interjected, "I tend to see things in ranges, for example, if you ask me about a new product I'd say it would sell 200,000 to 300,000 units in the price range of $10 to $12 a piece and each unit may cost us $6 to $9. Even in this simple example, even if you take extremes and the mid-point for each factor, you'd have 3x3x3, that is, 27 scenarios. If you use each of these scenarios, you'd have so many distinct numbers calculated for value. And if that's not complicated enough, there's the black box of discount rates."

## The Corporate Prophet

"That's a good point, Ony," continued Kathy, "I was about to get to the subject of how to use valuation for decision making. You do need to stress test your model. You do need to generate scenarios."

"In terms of Cash Flow, you can assign weightage to each scenario and work with weighted average Cash Flow."

"Discount rates are more complicated. When you are valuing a company, historical share price volatility gives some guidance, so does looking at the peers. In fact the scenarios themselves would provide some guidance on volatility of the weighted average Cash Flow."

"A robust way out is to adjust down your weighted average Cash Flow to account for risk and discount that Cash Flow by risk-free rate to account for the time value. You use appropriate government bond rate as the risk-free rate. In the end, as Kris mentioned, on any particular moment, for any particular transaction there's only one value."

"Well, not everything is traded on the stock market, how do you get around valuing those things?" King questioned. "For example, our internal R&D program."

"And," Hu added, "Given the fertile creative faculties you and your team have, you have no shortage of proposals fighting for funding. So there's no way you can avoid understanding the relative value of your current programs and proposals for future programs."

"So what we do," King nodded and continued, "is this."

"We ask ourselves if we can convert the idea to a useful product within a reasonable timeframe. We ask Ony to help us understand if the idea is going to be of any use to end users. Many of the ideas get filtered here."

"That's where we pitch in," Kathy interposed. "We continuously look at our financial condition to assess how much investment we can make in different areas. We do try to reasonably leverage our resources through various arrangements and partnerships; nevertheless we do not have infinite resources."

"Well, that sounds like an exaggeration. Demands for funds may be more than availability, but I don't think it's like infinite. I bet we are profitable enough and can repay our debt respectably." Henry sought clarification.

"Debt per se is not bad," Kris leaned forward taking support of the table.

"Lending and borrowing ensures that money gets to the place where it can be put to the most productive use. Borrowing as we all know is not free. At any point of time we compete with other people who are in need of funding and, depending on the demand and supply, we need to pay a price for the funds we borrow."

"Now, however, lenders would do business only when they have a reasonable belief on return of investment, even before they worry about return on investment. So they will assess if we would be able to pay the interest. Interestingly, the more interest you pay, less is the overall profitability, because you cannot keep passing the increased burden of interest to the customer indefinitely. It's connected. The more you borrow, the less is your ability to borrow further. So, naturally, there would be a limit."

"The other source of funding is equity. However, that means direct reduction of the relative stake of the shareholders and needs to be carefully considered. Again, anyone putting an equity stake would also be worried about the return. Different investors have different appetite for risk, so you should pitch to those whose risk-appetite is matching with your own risk-profile. There are no guarantees though. There are times when investor sentiment is weak and you may have to toil hard for funding in those times."

"You would borrow or issue equity if you have to, but with extreme caution and to the lowest extent possible."

"I understand that, but how do you explain our surplus fund kept in safe securities. Why don't we tap into that?" Hu was the one who asked this time.

Mohan Pandey

Kris stretched back and said in a relaxed tone, "We keep that for the rainy day. We have talked about all kinds of risks that businesses face. We need to keep some cushion to get through temporary setbacks, of our own doing or caused by extraneous factors. And, yes, we keep the fund safe because we don't want too much uncertainty when we are banking on that money in cases that they themselves are uncertain."

"If I go back to what I was saying," Kathy smiled and continued, "we need to worry not only about balancing the availability constraints, we need to worry about balancing funding our present and future as well. If the present is not funded well, there's no support for the future. But if the future is crowded out by the present, stakeholders won't like that either."

"So at any point of time we have proposals for investments to be made in branding, capacity creation, R&D etc. Another dimension is the requirement of stability in R&D investments. Thus, we kind of maintain a certain level of investment on a relatively longer time scale. Once the pool is decided, all I have to do is to look at King's list and see if all the shortlisted proposals can be funded. Invariably, requested money is way above the available pool. Nothing wrong with that as it shows our intellectual strength. What I do is to use the phase-wise technical probability of success and integrate that with marketing projections probability adjusted for different scenarios and calculate what is technically called Expected Net Present Value. Many a times, small investment proposals, by way of larger impact on portfolio, may have higher value. While at the same time, large investment proposals with low probability of success may not make it. Finally, it's not about blindly using a number. All this is presented to King's senior leadership team for strategic decision. King of course has the final decision on that."

"Very well", applauded Kris, "that's very well presented."

"When it comes to this stage we understand the proposal in its entirety. There are some proposals that very clearly appear to be winners. Some others would be on the fence—that can be debated. Valuation is a tool that helps you. You make the decision."

"Interestingly," King observed, "we do get good consensus after such meetings. And I must mention that our stated long-term commitment to innovation has helped us immensely in doing some great research."

Kris smiled, "my friend, innovation is the most potent engine of growth."

# 10. Innovation

"Creation makes us happy. Research brings us truth. Innovation is nothing but bringing creation and research together to do good, either by improving an existing solution or by finding a new solution. In the process, we add value. What do you think, King?" Kris stopped.

"Well, for some of us, research is an end in itself. The sheer joy of discovery is incomparable to anything else. However, the endeavor to discover things hitherto unknown comes with an inherent risk—the risk of failure. When we are trying something new, it may or may not work. Right from the assumptions, to the hypotheses, to the tools available to us at any point of time we might hit roadblocks. This uncertainty adds to the charm, the mystic of research. The challenge makes it more inviting." King's face brightened.

"Rewards are no less enticing," Kathy added, "if you bring out meaningful products and services and meet significant unmet needs. There's enough evidence to suggest that greater innovation intensity leads to greater economic prosperity."

Mohan Pandey

"While that's true," John pointed out, "if you do decide to walk this path you would need to persevere. At the same time, you need to know when enough is enough. You should know when to change tracks."

"Good point, John," Kris agreed, "the risk of failure is there. But then, no innovation means guaranteed failure."

"When we look at the risks involved, we oftentimes tend to think that one needs to be lucky to be a successful innovator. When we ask the experts, we're told that there's no defined process to increase the frequency of sparks popping up in ignited minds. These are the thoughts that would hold your feet as if your shoes were bolted to the earth. You don't need such shoes, untie your laces and run barefoot."

"Remember, serendipities help only those minds that are ready. Look around, reflect on the history of humanity and you'll see very clearly there have been times and places that stand out in terms of innovation. You'll notice a mountain with a peak called Archimedes, somewhere else, Aryabhatta and not too far away would be Ma Jun. You'll cross Ibrahim-ibn-Sina and would then be startled with close up of peaks of Galileo, Newton, Einstein and King."

King rolled his eyes.

Kris continued matter-of-factly.

## The Corporate Prophet

"At the end of this marvelous sojourn you would be amazed to find that innovations build on what exists as much as against what exists. Innovations flourish in times of peace and they bloom in times of war. You wouldn't miss this fact though, that whenever the candle of inquiry is blown off, the dark ages of stagnation follow."

"So, this is what you'd do to create an organization with high probability of success at innovation. You would have demonstrated long-term commitment to innovation. You would selectively attract the very best and deliberately create diversity. When you attract the best, you would also offer challenges commensurate to their faculties and in line with the needs of the end users. You would break the silos and encourage questioning."

"You'd build strong walls to protect your intellectual property, but you'd also have open windows."

"The urge to have uniform policy across your organization can be counterproductive. Parts of your organization should focus on exploitation of current knowledge and parts of your organization should focus on exploration. Be bold enough and create differentiated incentive plans."

"Incubate those who explore. For them you would structure the incentives that reward success but at the same time, you wouldn't punish failures caused by the inherent risks. You get better at it if you allow multiple rounds of exploration. Thus, you would be better off with a base plan for present and an upside associated with future success."

"Keep this in mind, every day when you walk into your lab, walk in with the belief that you'll discover something great that day. Many a times your discoveries may not be immediately understood, but if you don't believe in your work, no one else will."

"While it's clear that you need to have an environment that promotes innovation, is there anything we can do about increasing innovation competence?" Hu asked.

"Yes, you can," Kris responded. "And I'd let King share his thoughts on this."

"Sure," King was happy to talk about his pet subject, "start with hiring the right people."

"To some extent you can assess people's creation and innovation quotient by asking the right questions. Then you could spread the thinking, questioning process through structured training. There are some powerful tools developed in the past decades. People can be trained on that."

"With all that, I still feel, there's something within some people that makes them extremely creative. When I express this thought, some colleagues don't like that. Honestly though, I'm looking at this subject in a simple manner. For example, in athletics, some people can run faster than others can, some people can jump farther than others can, and some people can jump higher than others can. In the same way, some people are more creative than others." King concluded.

"Thanks King," Kris started, "with the benefit of the discussion so far, let me summarize how our task is cut out."

"As a leader of a research organization, your foremost task would be communicating, radiating and transferring the belief that you have in the organization to every member of the organization."

"As the senior leadership team of the company, your task would be ensuring that the research organization fits well with the overall system. It should work on the problems that are meaningful and you should be able to commercialize the output of research. In some cases, you'd have worked backwards from the existing customer need. In other cases, you'd have to be creative with what you get out of research and match that to an existing or potential need."

"Can I add something here?" John asked and started after a pause.

"Innovation is not limited to finding new products. We innovate when we discover a new process, when we discover a new system, when we put an existing thing to a new use, when we connect existing things in a new way, when we deconstruct an existing object in a new way, when we find a new business model, and so on. An innovative organization doesn't limit innovation within the four walls of a laboratory. Innovation permeates the organization. It becomes part of the culture."

"Would that not," Hu was still thinking when she started her statement, "I mean, would that not make the overall enterprise extremely risky? You see innovation is risky, more innovation then means more risk."

"That's an interesting thought," King jumped in.

"However, in line with what Kris described, lack of innovation is the bigger risk."

"Also," John said, "no one stops us from innovating in the area of risk management either."

"Well, that's part of the answer," Kris added, "but Hu's question deserves a complete response."

"If I understand you right, your worry is that if everyone, all the time, is tweaking with something, hypothetically speaking all systems would be in a perpetual flux. That would then mean zero implementation. This would certainly be value negative. Did I get your question right?"

"Yes. Finding new products and services to be sold to customers is fine. In addition, I understand that it's not about separating innovation from your day job. It's about innovating how to do your day job better. You read my mind right, I was worried about nothing ever getting implemented."

Kris nodded. "That's a valid point. We should remember that true innovation is not just about generating new ideas, it starts with an idea and innovation converts that idea to practical use, real value. An innovation culture would therefore increase value. It is pursuit of Truth in the end, of course, it should increase value."

"A culture of innovation coupled with Systems Thinking would ensure that increase in value in one pocket is not negative somewhere else. With that, I don't want to romanticize innovation. Indeed, innovation has risk as well as uncertainty but tell me one endeavor worth pursuing that doesn't have risk or uncertainty!"

# 11. Risk and Uncertainty

"Several events that we observe in the world can be predicted at a reasonable confidence level. There are ways to calculate and predict where you'd see a particular constellation or planet a year or ten years from now. You can also predict where a ball will land if you throw it in a certain direction. However, many events defy prediction. Some of them are not predicted well because of limitations of understanding of the system—things beyond the realms of our existing knowledge, tools of measurement or capacity of processing information. There are other cases that can be predicted to some extent but only in a statistical manner, for example, the time that it takes to drive through a city road, life expectancy, molecular motion etc. And, there are still others that are chaotic beyond a point, like weather, earthquakes, the stock market etc."

King was all excited with the mere mention of the word 'molecular'. "Individual molecular motion is intrinsically uncertain, but can be statistically understood in aggregate. Creative sparks of individuals is intrinsically unpredictable, but can be statistically understood for a group."

Mohan Pandey

"Hmm," Hu whispered, "it's completely unpredictable as to when King will open his mouth, but statistically the one time, out of twenty times, that he speaks, he's also understood."

"Hoo asked you to open your mouth?" King retorted.

"Simply put, there are three broad categories: unknown events, known events with known frequency, and known events with unknown frequency."

"There's nothing much you can do about the first category, the uncertainty; just accept that as a fact of life. For others you can apply some level of modeling and understand the risk involved, that's how far something may go from the value you expect and if it does how it's going to impact the proposition in question."

"Having developed an understanding you can deliberate on what you want to do about those risks. You should mitigate those that you can with reasonable investment of resources, for example, through insurance. Finally, you must provide for a contingency for the rest. We did touch upon this when Kathy was talking about Finance."

"The world is in a flux and thus the risk assessment should be done regularly and as in any good system, if you have mitigation action items, you should also have identified people who'd be responsible for those action items. Usually, risk is not the issue, poor risk management is."

"Remember though, that risk need not always be bad. In fact, things might turn out to be better than your expectations. You should always have a proactive plan to use such instances to your benefit."

"Absolutely," Hu jumped in, "the symbol for risk in Chinese represents loss and gain together."

"I learnt it the hard way", Ony adjusted himself in his chair, "there's nothing as risky as the market place, but then that's the only place where fortunes are made."

"True, Ony," Kris said turning toward him, "but it's no less true in the case of innovation. However, since we are on the subject, why don't you enlighten us a little more about the markets?"

# 12. Marketing and Sales

Ony closed his eyes and started enacting like a monk giving a sermon.

"A market is a place where goods and services are exchanged, albeit facilitated by this otherwise worthless instrument called money. The most important thing in a market is your understanding of your customer. And because of all the flux in this world, your customer is not a static being. So your understanding has to be as current as possible. Wrong understanding and your offering may get rejected. Lack of understanding and you may miss the next wave."

"Long ago in another life when I was promoted as the Vice President of Marketing and Sales for an electronic goods company, I delegated the task of gathering market related information on a new product to an external consultant. We received a thick bound report and the creative team came out with this brilliant tag line—'Aspire!'"

"Thankfully, as always, a pilot was done before taking a decision on the full launch; and it was a flop!"

"I was cursing myself as to why I outsourced the research. I promised myself that I'd make time to go and meet real customers in real time. One day, reflecting on this disaster, I remembered that not everyone in the planning meeting had whole-heartedly supported the plan. One of them was an intern. The next day, I went up to her desk and asked her what she thought went wrong. She was a little bit hesitant initially, but then she mentioned that there was nothing wrong with the consultant's report, but the country where we piloted the promotion had moved into an austerity drive and we should have been mindful of that."

"On another occasion, I missed an opportunity of offering my key product in a variety of colors. 'Model T' mistake all over again. I woke up when our closest competitor had gotten there first and had gained an additional five percentage points in market share."

"I'm proud," Kris commented, "that we have people like Ony who can openly share their failures. Also, no one knows more than I do, that he learnt from all his mistakes."

"You may not know, but one day, he walked into my office and said 'Marketing is too important for a CEO to delegate down' and he convinced me to spend at least one fourth of my time meeting with customers directly. He spends half of his own time doing that. The intern in his story was none else but our Jane, who we all know has only one passion, talking to customers."

# The Corporate Prophet

"That's where we start, but then, a lot happens after that. Why don't you continue your sermon, monk?"

Ony was in no mood to stop anyway.

"I see it as a reflexive process. As much as we need to educate customers about our products and services, we need to learn from them what kind of products and services they need. We co-create and co-evolve."

"For any product or service, we assign a name to simplify communication with our existing and potential customers. We then develop a personality for the name so that customers can recall it despite the environment being cluttered with overload of information. We continuously reinforce the personality with various communications and associations. With such efforts, a customer starts to associate some value with the name, the product, the service. That then defines the expected value."

"We also carefully try to convert that expected value on a monetary scale—how much is the customer willing to pay. Here it gets tricky. What we want to maximize is the total value that the product or service brings to the company. Too high a price, not many customers, lost economies of scale and we suffer. Too low a price, large volumes, but inadequate margin and we suffer."

"Voodoo", King quipped.

Mohan Pandey

"Well, there may be an element of subjectivity here. However, unless we are talking of an out of the world new idea, we would have reasonable benchmarks to look at. We look around and fish for other means through which similar needs are fulfilled. That way we understand a range. Then we try to see what additional value we bring, and understand where on that map we should be."

"Well, you could always go up or down in terms of price", Hu reasoned.

"Absolutely, firms do increase or decrease price. That's a very sensible thing to do, but for one little problem. If you decrease the price, some customers may feel cheated. I must emphasize the word 'feel'. There are real cases where increased sales allow us to enhance economies of scale and pass the benefit on to customers, which leads to a genuine decrease in price. So, what I advocate is start a little lower compared to what you think is the right price."

"Is that good from the shareholders' perspective?" Kathy looked worried.

"It probably is," responded Ony, "as we just discussed, the overall value is important. If through this minor sacrifice, we're ensuring that our customer's expected value is close to the price, or even favorable to our customer, we would have customers coming back to us. And, very importantly, the customer would then spread the good word around. So overall, we benefit."

"And then, you get to deliver the goods," the Operations man jumped in.

Ony smiled, "If the price paid doesn't match the actually realized value you are doomed. Sales is not just transactional, when you sell something to someone, you are starting a relationship."

"You need to ensure that the product works as per customer's expectations, in fact, if you want to survive in today's competitive market, you should rather exceed customer's expectations. One is not talking of the mere functionality of product or service here; it's the whole experience—how easy it was to buy, how good the follow up was. So you need to have a great sales team backed by an excellent distribution platform that ensures the balance of the chain."

"If I may summarize, marketing is neither voodoo nor rocket science. You need to understand both your offering and the potential customers and existing customers in real terms. You need to build a brand systematically and create the desire in your customer to buy. You ensure that your product and service is easily accessible and the necessary after-sales support is truly in place. You price your product close to the perceived value and deliver higher actual value compared to the price paid by the customer. Of course, launch it only if

Mohan Pandey

it's going to be value positive for the company. Finally, be bold, take reasonable risks, otherwise you'd never launch a product."

"End-to-end, you need to get the whole strategy right," Ony said. "No strategy in the world will be successful if you don't have the right people," Hu finished.

# 13. People

"I absolutely agree with that," Kris said.

"No strategy in world can be successful if you don't have the right people. Now that's not something that you didn't know. If you're developing software, you need somebody who can write a program. If you want to run a reaction, you need a chemist who knows how to set a reaction up. People must have the skill set for them to do their job. Yet just being round doesn't make an object a wheel."

"A wheel needs to be strong, strong enough to carry the desired load. It needs to have features that connect it to the cart. Then it needs to be able to negotiate with the road with just about the right kind of attachment and detachment that allows it to handle the road when it is smooth or when it is uneven. A wheel also needs to be in the right proportion to the other wheels, as well as to the cart."

Hu interrupted, "Kris, but human beings are not inanimate like a wheel, they have a brain and a heart, and they have relationships and identities."

"Absolutely so", replied Kris, "and that is why you don't have a formula written for predicting human behavior. However, there are some useful steps that we can take to ensure that we are right more often than wrong."

"Yes, the first thing", commented Hu, "is getting the right CEO." She looked around to see if everyone agreed, and indeed, they did.

"Well, that's the most important job the Board has to do. If you're starting or running your enterprise, it's you who's in the hot seat. Yet it's not only about this one position, it's about all the positions. Members of the organization are not merely economic entities, nor is the relationship just economic. As an organization we should be able to clearly define and communicate to the members their, and others', roles, responsibilities, and accountabilities. I mean right from the beginning of the relationship, that is, recruitment."

"Be rigorous so that the organization is able to decide if the candidate fits the organization. Do remember that it is not a one-sided deal, nor a one-time transaction. Early interactions go a long way and they need to stand on a foundation of trust."

Kathleen controlled herself from interrupting, but then she jumped in. "Well, Kris, don't you think it's about the demand and supply of the required skill sets in the labor market?"

Kris reflected for a moment or two. "There's nothing wrong with that view. It's indeed consistent with the mainstream assumptions of economics. The problem is we aren't that rational, at least, there are times when we aren't rational. We're not happy when we're poor, but are we happy when we're rich? But even from the perspective of labor markets, the markets have a certain stickiness and once you factor in the long term overall value maximization instead of instantaneous gains out of the fluctuations in the labor market, it's clear that we cannot have a transactional view of the relationship a organization has with it members."

Kathy asked, "Aren't you mixing personal and professional?"

John was off even before Kathy's sentence finished. "This kind of separation, you know Kathy, has made us all schizophrenic, split lives."

Kris supported John. "How relevant is it for us to compartmentalize our life? Should we think of ourselves as having multiple identities, or should we consider a single identity that's made of many dimensions? After all a rose in pink soft and fragrant, all at the same time. So is a mango—yellow, supple and sweet. Is it that I cease to be your colleague when I'm playing with my son? Or, I cease to be a father when I'm in office?"

"In a utopian society, people would be doing exactly what they want to do and that would also pay for their bills. Now, however, not doing anything at all or doing things that don't add value to others is not going to be productive, because no one would barter his or her valuables with something of no value. Thus, in the world that we live in, we need to find an area of work that we reasonably like and an organization where we feel motivated enough to contribute. Turn it around and we go back to the same point we discussed, that is, we need to ensure the right fit."

"And Trust. Trust is the most magical thing I've ever seen in my practice of business. It always adds value. In terms of economics, it reduces the transaction costs. At a subtler level, it reduces risk. Reduction in risk increases value." And he looked at Kathy.

"Sure", Kathy nodded, "But Kris, there's more to the art of managing people, beyond recruitment. Why don't you talk about that too?"

Kris turned to Hu, "Why don't you share some of the secrets from your basket?"

Hu smiled, "No secrets really, we practice these things regularly in our organization. There are processes in place for all the interactions that members have with the organization—hire to retire (and beyond that). Yet as much as we rely on processes, we put people first. We treat people with fairness. Compensation is linked to value addition, and that applies across the organization. Then we respect each individual and we make it very clear that respect is a basic creed of the organization. We believe that, in general, people don't wake up every

The Corporate Prophet

morning thinking how to destroy value. People want to do good, we enable them in that pursuit. We provide work environment that's not only comfortable, but beautiful as well. While people can differ on policies, strategies and plans, we expect them to be true to the fundamental values. Values that Kris has put CRISPly".

Collaboration. Respect. Integrity. Sustainability. Positivity.

They shared a quick smile as they recalled the office joke that 'collaboration' should be spelled as 'kollaboration'. King, who had stepped out for a leak, walked in asking, "Looks like I missed the joke." One more round of laughter followed. It was well known that King needed to take a break every hour or so.

"Guess it was KRISP! You know what; we talk so much about people, the value they bring and such things. Yet, when a company announces a layoff, the share price goes up. I've never been able to reconcile that."

"That's an interesting observation," Kris reflected. "Let's spend some time on this."

"The value of your company is not of the company in isolation, but is the value that it generates by playing its role in this interconnected world. The fluctuations in your stock price do indicate changes that you

Mohan Pandey

go through internally, but also the changes that are external to you and nevertheless impacting your potential to create value. But coming to the particular point that King made, lay off in a way is admitting that the existing organizational structure doesn't derive value from those people who are being laid off. Many a times, it could just be a technological wave that makes the skill sets of many people redundant. There could be situations when you build up a workforce in anticipation of a certain demand, and then you were proven wrong. And there are yet other times when mergers of organizations lead to redundancy of certain roles. But in all these cases, stock markets essentially see lay-offs as reduction in cost base, and that's how the value goes up."

"If there's one reason why organizations have to be extremely cautious in creating and filling positions it is this risk of lay-offs. They should also be proactive in helping people maintain their relevance, and even beyond, in finding new ways of enhancing opportunities of value enhancement. And as much as that is true, we should all stand up as individuals and take ownership of our careers."

# 14. Managing Self

Kris always had time for everyone and everything, or so went the legend. For a fact, it was well known that he was well organized, and had an extremely efficient assistant to help him. No one ever felt rushed when they met Kris. Kris never fiddled with his smartphone during meetings. On top of all this, he always took his vacations and spent a lot of time with his family.

Kris continued, "It starts with you. You are not the centre of the world; nevertheless, you indeed are the centre of your world. In any case, if it's your journey, the steps have to be yours."

"You have, all of us have, the same twenty four hours in a day. We may choose to drift with time or we may choose to take control. Not for a moment am I suggesting that any of us are or can be in control of the Universe. However, we are not a mere fallen feather pushed around by the powerful stream of events; we are active players. To the extent we can act, we need to take charge. Don't view yourself as a victim or a victor; we are not at war with the World, we engage with it, we immerse in it, and we co-create history."

Mohan Pandey

"Frankly Kris, there are tomes written on time management, but we still seem to struggle in that area." Henry commented.

"Well, for that matter, there are tomes written on almost everything," quipped Kris, smiling mischievously, "and still, most of the time, we don't do the right things; knowing is one thing, using that knowledge is another."

"No, I'm not going to talk about managing time. You cannot manage Time. You have to manage yourself."

"Of course, that'll mean that you would make a list of items that you personally need to work on, you would assess time requirement for each activity, you would assess importance and urgency of activities and you would schedule them on your calendar accordingly. That's but just one part of the puzzle."

"Much like an organization, human beings too need to first define their objectives and the higher purpose. If you're doing something, it should be worth doing. In my experience, most of the things worth doing do not need any explicit reason. You climb Mt. Everest because it's there. You go to the Moon because it's there. You stand up for Truth because you cannot live any other way. You admire Beauty because you cannot not admire. You create good, because you just feel like doing it. Remember the Triad. When you have that kind of motivation from inside, you can move mountains."

Ony, who was silent for a while now, broke his silence in his unique way, "Well on the ground, the problem is this; how do we discover our purpose and how do we define the same?"

"Thanks for bringing me back from the mountains," chuckled Kris.

"Here's one idea that you are familiar with.

"Imagine the day when you finally hang your boots; imagine when you reflect back on your life, how would you feel that day? What will you tell yourself? If you're able to tell yourself that it was a life well spent, my friends, you've done it."

"What about our family, the society, their expectations of us?" Kathy asked.

Kris replied, "You're not going to be able to fool yourself that you have done great if that apparent greatness was achieved at the expense of your family or friends. Don't change the frame of reference though. The same object looks different if you change the perspective. Keep with one perspective, otherwise there are practically infinite perspectives and venturing into that kind of analysis will paralyze you. You have to do an honest job yourself, for yourself. If you've done something worthwhile, it will benefit many others for sure. That's how superlative goals are. By no means do I want to undermine the perspectives others have, at least some key people in your life will be able to help you with this exercise. Get input; get feedback, that's useful. All I'm saying is this; if you've not accomplished what you truly wanted to accomplish, there is nothing else that can fill in; and, whatever you have accomplished is nothing if you have failed on the family front."

"Well, in our offsite meeting last year, you made all of us work on our retirement speeches. Your first idea of preparing our own obituaries was way too dark for us to digest. But I guess it was a very useful exercise," John recalled.

Kris just nodded and continued, "Then ask yourself, what is it that you need to do between today and that day to be able to eventually have a feeling of life well spent. Pick two to five key long-term goals. Break them down into medium term and short-term goals. Also, write down clearly how you propose to achieve those goals and in doing so what are the values that would guide you. Repeat this exercise once every year."

"One caution though; don't fall into the trap of becoming completely one-dimensional. Be aware of the higher spiritual plane, be aware of social and family responsibilities, be aware of obligations to achieve your potential and then, also be aware of your obligations to yourself. Carnal desires are not be suppressed. Enjoy life, but not at the cost of the others. Just so that there is a balance, let me mention that there's no limit to those desires, adding more oil doesn't extinguish the fire. It's oftentimes observed that items that aren't good for us come packaged in attractive covers. Don't become a slave to your cravings. Extremes are edgy, be balanced."

"Your body is the vehicle through which you accomplish whatever you want to accomplish. Manage your health actively. Set aside some meaningful time for physical exercise. A healthy mind resides in a healthy body, but don't take it for granted. The more complicated the problems that you put your mind to, the stronger it becomes. Also, train your mind so that it's in your control. Pick your tool, music, mantras or meditation—whatever—but don't let it run wild on adrenaline. Whenever you're in situations that your mind starts to get out of your control, step back, think, and only then act. Because, when your mind is not in control, you lose your ability to distinguish the bad from the good. Not only do you lose clarity of vision, you also become shortsighted. And any action taken in such a state would lead to results that are not good for you and in many instances may put you in a vicious spiral or even make situations completely chaotic."

"One question that has always bugged me," said King, "is about the importance of grooming."

"If I'm good at what I do, is it important to spend my valuable time on dressing up every day?"

Mohan Pandey

"Guess what, I'm wearing mismatched socks today!" said Kris.

"That's something," Kathy was shocked. Kris was always immaculately dressed and people admired his sartorial sense. So this was indeed unusual.

"Well, this is only the second time it's happened, the first time was on my first day in office", Kris shrugged and continued.

"There are three aspects of grooming. One is the hygiene part of it. I don't think there's any doubt that we need to maintain ourselves properly to avoid falling sick and to ensure that we aren't a nuisance to people around us. The second part is about economics, though a higher price doesn't necessarily mean better style. Lastly, it's about aesthetics, and how you carry what you wear; and that's completely a matter of personal choice and attitude. Unless there's a professional need, for example, wearing safety glasses and aprons when you go to your lab, you could be wearing anything you like. However, you should also be aware of your environment and respectful of the culture around you. Your appearance is the first signal that anyone meeting with you receives, and you should know how to utilize appearance as a communication tool."

"Your physical appearance is part of your own branding. Like all other great brands, eventually you have to deliver on your promises consistently. Some of us are high on promise and low on delivery, that's no good. Even those who are high on delivery and low on communication may miss some opportunities. You have to project yourself through your contributions. So strike a balance. Do and say. You're your own brand ambassador."

"In my experience," added Henry, "your being conscious about yourself significantly improves how you deal with others."

# 15. Managing Others

"That's absolutely true," Kris connected with Henry, "and is extremely important."

"Usually, the achievement of your end objectives doesn't depend on your solitary effort. You have to work with others to be successful. You have your superiors, peers and juniors within your organization; and suppliers and customers outside of your organization, and you need to work effectively with all of them."

"Truth within manifests as Trust outside."

"It's this one factor of Trust that's the secret of managing others. You build trust by being honest, consistent, respectful and fair."

"Be honest in saying 'No', if you cannot deliver on something. When you say 'Yes', then leave no stone unturned to fulfill your promise. While it's good to ask 'What's in it for me?' it's important enough to lay out 'What's in it for you?'"

"Communicate as much as you can, and be consistent. You may be required to keep some information confidential; however, don't have any hidden agenda. If you cannot share something, say so, don't give out false information."

"Respect others. If you can do everything by yourself, you wouldn't need a team. If you can manage everything within, you wouldn't need any supplier. Everyone in an optimized value chain has some value to add. Respect them for that. Most importantly though, respect everyone as fellow human beings."

"Compensate in a fair manner. By that, I mean, anyone who's helping you in meeting your objective deserves a fair compensation. And, you'd rather exceed expectations."

"Wow, that's so simple and clear," Hu was excited.

"Indeed so, but as Kris mentioned, knowing is one thing, practicing is another," shrugged Ony.

"Hmm, but your journey, your steps," John emphasized.

"Can I bring another perspective here?" Henry paused and continued.

"Mostly in dealing with others, we're usually bogged down by mundane issues like, how do I ask for more resources, how do I delegate, how do I motivate others, how do I ask for a raise and so on. Kris, you have dealt with all sorts of such things. How do you do that?"

"Thanks Henry," Kris started, "for bringing this very practical aspect."

"The basic principles are the same, but let me illustrate with some examples from the situations you mentioned. That's how I see them, as situations and not as problems. Asking for a raise is probably the most debated situation. A great organization should have systems to address this proactively in a fair manner so that there would be no need for anyone to ask for a raise. The question here is how would you ask if you have to ask?"

"First, be fair to yourself, ask if you deserve a raise. Your current compensation was decided based on market realities and in proportion to the value you bring to the organization. Has the market changed? Has the magnitude of your contribution changed? What's the evidence? How do you quantify that?"

"If you're convinced with your case, move to the next step. If you know that your organization encourages such discussion only at certain period or periods in a year, wait for the appropriate time and follow the process. In general, you should inform your superior that you want to have this discussion. Send her your case summary in advance with your calculations. Let her have some time to evaluate. Go with an open mind, understand her viewpoint. She may know something that you do not. Since you are a person known to be honest and a person that she trusts already, most likely it'll be a good discussion. You have the best chance of getting a raise this way."

"If you don't succeed in getting a raise this way, you've probably understood the scenarios in which you might deserve a raise, that is, from your superior's perspective. Maybe you need to gain additional skills or experiences. Create a plan for that."

"If you're still not convinced and you think you'd be valued higher in another organization, then don't feel shy in evaluating that as well. If you're sure that the total true value of movement is more than the total true cost of movement, go ahead make the move. Don't burn your bridges though, and if you've been honest, people will understand why you moved and there wouldn't be any hard feelings."

"What's this 'total true cost' business?" Ony raised his hand.

"It's means ensuring that you account for tangible and intangible, monetary and non-monetary benefits and costs. For example, your growth prospects, cost of moving your family, commute time etc." Kathy explained. "Kris and I have discussed similar lines during our corporate finance discussions of acquisitions, investments etc. We could credit him with the concept of tNPV, the true Net Present Value."

"Honestly, the phrase is yours," Kris turned to Kathy, "all I mean is that when you look at NPV look at it holistically and honestly."

"Can we discuss one more example?" Henry was not willing to allow any diversion of the discussion,

## The Corporate Prophet

"I understand concepts better when such examples are used."

"Of course," Kris continued, "let's talk about a case where you want a junior colleague of yours to take up a challenging yet risky assignment. To make it little difficult, let's say your organizational policies don't allow you to offer material benefits over and above the current pay he's getting."

"Again, the first step is within. You need to believe in the cause before you can motivate others to join you in your journey. So be very clear in terms of what you want to be achieved. Think through the proposition and make an honest case. Don't offer unhealthy inducements; don't make promises that cannot be fulfilled."

"Prepare for the conversation. Many a times, the biggest error is assuming that you know everything and that you'll be able to articulate everything properly during your conversation. I'm not saying that you need to script out everything and act the conversation. I'm also not suggesting that you spend time in creating a logical maze to trap somebody. It's not deception; it's preparation. It's about respecting the person with whom you're going to interact. It's about respecting the time you're going to spend and the other person is going to spend. Without any doubt, for important interactions you should prepare for an honest structured conversation."

Mohan Pandey

"As you start the discussion, articulate the objective very clearly. That takes a minute or two. Then explain the nature of the assignment and the benefits to the organization. Elaborate the reason behind the selection of this particular person for this assignment. Since you trust this person, express your confidence that he'll do a good job. Pause and ask if he understands you."

"Keep enough time for clarifications. You should be able to illustrate how such challenging assignments add value to profiles. If the person is hesitant, probe to understand the reason. There may be valid reasons that you didn't know; for example, at that point he may not be able to travel, though the assignment requires frequent travel. Also, offer to enable him with all the tools that he would need; though it's important to clarify that you are enabling, but he's going to do the job."

"If it's appropriate, give him time to think and revert. In the end, it's very likely that your judgment of selecting this person was correct and the person will feel motivated to take up the assignment. However, even if that doesn't happen, you'd understand the person much better and you wouldn't have forced a disaster upon him, yourself and your organization."

"Those are good examples," Hu commented, "and I think you can utilize this model for pretty much any scenario."

The Corporate Prophet

"However, Kris, would you mind spending some time on something that's extremely important for all of us—Managing performance?"

"Thanks Hu," Kris responded, "it's very important to have an efficient system to manage performance and for all the managers to know how to manage performance."

"You first need to start with Objective Setting. Objectives should percolate down from the overall organizations goals and should be clearly defined and communicated. These clear organizational objectives should be built upon vision as well as the current reality. So have a system that allows integration of unfiltered ground level feedback into the organizational objective formulation. The process should also allow you to assess, provide feedback and modify the objectives as needed due to changes in internal and external environment."

"Once the top level objectives are clearly laid out they should be supported by functional or project level objectives which in turn should be supported by individual objectives. These sub-level objectives should be aligned with top-level objectives and should be optimized to remove duplication of effort. That can be achieved through a good alignment discussion. In the end, the individuals should agree that the objectives are structured in a way that they are specific and measurable and of such magnitude that's achievable. Also, they should do justice to the frequency of assessment. As an organization, your system should allow periodicity of assessment to be appropriate for the objective in question."

"Rewards should be aligned with performance. A system that doesn't allow high performance to be rewarded differentially would suck out the motivation of the high performers and the organization would lose out to those systems that attract them."

"The reward is not always monetary, if it suits your organizational culture, you may offer recognition or satisfaction as reward. Whatever the currency be, you should differentiate. This is not to say that you value others less. This is not about differentiating one human being from another. No. All human beings are equal. What you need to establish is that a particular person's contribution to the organization in a particular period is differentiated as compared to others. Otherwise, we create inefficiencies that would be detrimental to the whole organization in the long run."

"Since I did mention that you should have opportunity to change the objectives if needed, it's imperative to ensure that you don't punish people for failures that were reasonably beyond their control. However, keep the incentives aligned with achievements."

"That's about the system. However, for all us, performance management is not a periodic exercise. It's a daily job. Take the opportunity, as you go, to provide feedback whenever you see someone in your group isn't doing so well, applaud out of the ordinary work and prepare your people continuously for higher challenges as you coach them regularly."

"It'll happen only when you're genuinely interested in developing your people. That genuine interest will reflect in everything else that you do for them. And that's when they will be genuinely interested in learning."

# 16. Learning

"The crop of intellect is abundant and is all around us. However, you have to harvest it for yourself, and prepare it for consumption. Then, as you chew and swallow those morsels, you get nourished. Once you are nourished, you go back to the fields and prepare them anew wherein old strains and new strains merge and new crops flourish in abundance."

"We can and do learn from what is out there already. Also, we can and do learn from our unique perspectives, thinking, experimenting and experience. Both these dimensions are important. There's no point in reinventing the proverbial wheel—the same wheel. However, there's a lot to gain in thinking about the wheel from a different perspective. You could always ask yourself even such simple questions like, 'What's a wheel? 'What's the function of a wheel?' 'How does a wheel work?' 'Can the same objective be achieved in a different way?' 'Can a wheel's functionality be enhanced?' And so on."

"When you ask these questions afresh, remember that you should have a reasonable understanding of what's already known. It's like creating a scaffold—you stand on what is built, and then build the next level."

"While you'd like to know all that is out there, balance this between the time you invest in gathering that knowledge and thinking afresh. For sure, there's more out there than what we can ever digest. And, for sure, there's more out there that's not known than all that we know today."

"Nevertheless, you should know where to look for when you need to."

"So what percent of turnover, or of profits, should one invest in learning?" A trademark Kathy question.

"That depends on an organization's objectives," Kris started answering, "and the gap in the existing level of knowledge and the desired level of knowledge to meet those objectives."

"So you're actually saying that at some point of time you can stop investments in learning?" John exclaimed.

"Well, if the organization's objective is to die, it may as well do that," Kris had a mischievous smile on his face.

"Got 'a bro'," John immediately responded to his pal, "objectives evolve, and there are always long-term objectives at the interplay of aspiration and realism, and therefore, there's a continuous need to learn."

Kris gave him a thumbs-up.

# The Corporate Prophet

"I guess we need to understand the two key aspects of learning: individual's learning and development and an organization's learning and development." Hu commented.

"Absolutely," Kris supported her, "why don't you elaborate on this little more?"

"Sure, I'd be happy to," Hu continued.

"One basic element is that of an individual's own level of skills and expertise that's needed to perform any desired task. In any given environment if you have such resources available from the temples of learning outside you'd need to probably bridge the gap some bit. In case the gap is too wide, you may need to create some internal program to upgrade the skills. Again, you would design the program keeping in mind the capacity of your people to absorb the knowledge they are being soaked into."

"There are some skills acquired over a period of time, in general we use the phrase 'experience' for that. You could accelerate that somewhat, but not too much. Of course, I'm not talking of the outliers here."

"I tend to map these individual skills on two interconnected dimensions. 'Cognitive skills' and 'Applied skills'."

"Cognitive skill is about how you think, how you observe the world, how you absorb information, how you process information and how you frame your response to any situation."

"Applied skills convert your cognition to action. Here again I capture a variety of stuff where your action depends largely on yourself as the technical skills. The other element is how an individual works with others, as part of a team, as a junior, as a peer or as superior; even as we have learnt there are our attributes as a supplier or as a customer that can be improved. I call them social skills."

"We have a process wherein our learning facilitators work with all the managers to identify learning needs for everyone, vis-à-vis the organizational objectives. They also help in identifying appropriate interventions, administering those interventions and monitoring progress. In some cases, progress can be quantitatively tracked while in some cases, you're able to assess in a qualitative manner."

"Of course, I don't think we have a perfect system yet; but then, we are continuously working on it to improve it. And, thanks Kathy for supporting this whole endeavor with the appropriate budget." Hu stopped.

"Well, the case was clear to me, with these interventions we've been able to deliver on our promise adding to our revenues, and in many other cases people have come back with ideas to reduce costs. I won't be

## The Corporate Prophet

too off, if I said, our learning program has more than paid for itself," said Kathy.

"Cannot agree more," King supported this, "in an environment when others were cutting on learning, we actually gained a competitive advantage by pushing ahead with our learning program. It helped us build so many unique programs with universities and institutes all over and we did some great science."

"Thanks King," Hu continued, "the other and more subtle dimension is organizational learning."

"As Kris described in the beginning, organizations evolve. Evolution indeed, is a process of learning that gets embedded in the organization's fabric. Individuals learn. However, over a long period, we also have people joining and leaving the organization. Despite that churning, organizations that learn become more and more adapted to the emerging environment, and become more competitive."

"You would, without any doubt, need some degree of stability in the organization if you want any tacit individual knowledge to transfer to the next generation. This would be achieved by actively identifying and stabilizing those pockets. The next step is to identify and associate people who are capable enough of carrying forward and enriching that knowledge. The last step is a continuous exercise to codify knowledge to the extent that's practically possible. As we learn more and as new

Mohan Pandey

tools become available, what was completely tacit yesterday may be amenable to be made partially explicit today. The organization should provide the right incentives to make this happen on a continuous basis. Nevertheless, the manuals and the process maps should not make life more complicated than before. It should not hinder creative thinking. Yesterday's road maps may not be good enough for tomorrow's landscape."

"That's a nice way of looking at the subject," King added thoughtfully. "Science, of course, is a creative process. Nevertheless, if you look at it closely, we have so many protocols, processes and systems developed over centuries codified so well for the apprentices as well experts to tap into. All the protocols have clearly defined objectives, materials and methods accurately described, and observation and interpretation provided. All the experiments also document materials, methods, results, analysis and interpretation. This is all carefully archived in the laboratory notebooks, and which are all now electronic—safe and searchable—courtesy Henry. And, one experiment leads to another."

"In a world where we actually manufacture great products that we make available to our customers across the continents we cannot even function without organizational codified learning. We clearly map our processes with causal flow, linked with time, on X-axis and involved people or groups on Y-axis. Such maps also help us in continuously improving the processes by removing all the waste from the system. And, in my experience, all sorts of 'waiting' and 'redundancies' are the key culprits of making processes inefficient. We continuously exercise and keep burning that fat."

"Inevitably, because things keep changing, we have to keep exercising continuously." John added. His discipline of hitting the gym everyday for two hours was showing up clearly.

"You bring us to another interesting subject, John. In the end, the knowledge and learning needs to be embodied into some product or service that your customer values," Kris said. "So let us talk about that now, but before that let us applaud Hu for such a lucid explanation of one of the most complicated concepts that you can think of."

Everyone joined in the quick applaud that left Hu overwhelmed.

# 17. Production and Delivery

"How you set up your production organization decides how efficient it'll be. Structure is strength."

"On one extreme you have specialization and on another you have generalization. Specialization is supposed to increase individual productivity. Generalization is supposed to increase a team's flexibility."

"On one extreme is mass production and on another is personalized production. Mass production minimizes cost. Personalized production maximizes satisfaction."

"On one extreme is full vertical integration of raw material production to finished goods production and on another is a fully distributed model wherein you don't own even a single piece of the production chain. Full integration maximizes control and full distribution minimizes investment."

"On one extreme, you can produce everything at a single location and distribute it across the world and on another you can have production units all over the world. A single location will give significant economy of scale, while multiple locations will help in distribution and connect with customers."

Mohan Pandey

"As you can imagine, it's not an either/or situation, there could be numerous models generated out of the interaction of these dimensions. And surely, there are more dimensions that would be specific to the business you're in. The model you design and select may itself be a great source of competitive advantage. Once you're clear of your value proposition and objectives, you can reduce this question into an optimization problem. Obviously, if you've framed it right it would generate some options of which you can pick one based on your judgment."

"Isn't an optimization run supposed to generate one option so that you avoid this subjective element of 'judgment'?" Hu asked, and hurried to add, "Well, not that I know Maths that well!"

"I'm not ruling that out," Kris elaborated, "however, in a complex multi-factorial analysis, I'd expect more than one solution."

"For example, when you solve a simple quadratic equation you get two answers." Henry jumped in, "then you say that since the number of apples cannot be negative so the other answer, which is a positive number, is correct. You mean that kind of stuff, right?"

"Yes, that's a good way of looking at it." Kris looked happy.

"Now, having selected the structure, you need to ensure that the structure works efficiently. This is an ongoing process. Your output would be constrained by the bottleneck in the system. So you'd ensure that the whole chain is balanced accordingly, otherwise you'd end up seeing a lot of wastage that'll manifest in the form of increasing work-in-progress inventory. If there's a need to increase production you would add resources at the bottleneck first. As you remove the bottleneck from one place, it'll appear at another. Also, the demand from the marketplace might be fluctuating—sometimes dramatically—so you'd integrate your production with demand assessment."

"In an ideal world, you should be able to produce at exactly the same rate at which the demand generates and you'd be able to fulfill the same in zero time. In the real world, however, you need to balance and have some sort of inventory so that you can deliver to the customer in an acceptable time frame. The same principle applies whether it is production of physical goods or services. While you can model and minimize inventory, remember that it's easy to forget the customer while you're focusing on your computer. As long as everyone in the chain thinks about the customer, you'll have a self-organized system that is efficient. To ensure this, you should have appropriate forums for everyone to connect as well as the appropriate incentive systems."

"Can I add a note of caution," John said thoughtfully, "this 'thinking about customer' should be based on the correct information that's available through the chain with integrity. It's known that even a minor change at the last point transaction gets progressively exaggerated as it flows through to wholesaler, to the manufacturer and eventually to the supplier. It's a remarkable example of the butterfly effect."

"Good that you mentioned that, John," Kris said.

"One can always overdo something. That's a problem. However, the key insight that you provide isn't about overdoing; it's about fundamental issues with our comprehension and our interpretation. So you're right, it gets exponentially magnified as the number of nodes in the chain increase."

"You should strive to reduce the number of nodes as much as you would continuously strive to reduce and eliminate waste from the system. Using more material than what's necessary, using more time than what's necessary, letting material wait in the system, and even letting minds rust are all types of waste that you should continuously identify and actively eliminate."

"It's very likely that you would be entering into a multitude of partnerships to access the resources available outside of your organization. It may be a matter of capability or capacity. Those external relationships can be flexible like a supplier or rigid like a joint venture. Whatever is the case you should treat partners as equals and understand that they are important parts of the eco-system. They need to thrive if you have to. Beyond a question of survival, if you build relationships based on trust you would be creating a system that's more innovative and more responsive to the need of the customer and the changing environment."

"You should strive to build methods that are robust; so that quality is built-in. After-the-fact inspection can help you identify and remove defective items, but is inefficient. So you should target zero-defect and continuously monitor your quality chart to capture signals of deeper malaise. You need to empower people on the floor to present ideas for improvement. You should empower teams to carry out an honest analysis of the root-cause to make fundamental improvements, whether in terms of infrastructure, processes, or people."

"You should also be wise enough, again, to look at the system in entirety and link various symptoms to underlying issues through a careful use of principle of causality."

"This essentially goes back to how you think," King added. "Critical structured honest thinking, being able to probe—Why? Why? Why? Therefore? Therefore? Therefore? What then? What then? What then? And, I must say, this same approach is useful in all scenarios in life."

Mohan Pandey

"So true," Ony said, "though a different set of questions that I ask helps me in ensuring that whatever we plan actually gets done."

## 18. Execution

"Getting things done!" Kris reflected, "So often leaders forget about this."

"And those are the leaders who are soon forgotten. Execution is not an inferior task compared to, say, strategizing. Strategy connects the vision with the reality, and execution connects the strategy with the results."

"So what are those questions that help you getting things done?" Kris turned to Ony.

"The first is 'How?'" Ony responded.

"This means getting a logical structure and steps and broken down to a level that can be assigned to someone."

"To what extent though do you break? It might become a never-ending exercise." Henry expressed his concern.

Kris, who was looking at something beyond the window very intently, suddenly burst out, "Aha!"

"Sorry Ony, can I respond to Henry? Something just occurred to me while I was looking at the traffic outside."

"Oh sure, we are in for a gem, I guess." Ony smiled.

Mohan Pandey

Kris thanked him and started, "When we start from our home to come to the office, we make a plan in our minds. Car, fuel, route, keys etc. Also, we are intrinsically tuned to change our route, call the helpline, seek help etc., if needed. Nevertheless, we never plan at what exact speed we would be driving. We let that be guided by the state of the traffic, because that's highly uncertain. We also never create a detailed plan for refilling gas. That's the kind of work you intuitively know or have enough experience in. At what speed you move in any project cannot be predetermined completely. You would prepare as per the objectives, but also get started without waiting for one hundred percent information. You would breakdown the work into smaller units, but stop at a level where you are comfortable enough."

He immediately shifted gear, "so what's the next critical question, Ony?"

"The next one is 'Who?'" Ony, started as if nothing had happened in between.

"I ask, 'Who is going to get this done?' I'm not just asking for a name. I need to understand if I have people with the right capabilities and in right numbers to support my plan. If not, I'd rather go back and develop people or, depending on the need, hire people before starting with my plan."

"Finally, 'When?' What's the sequence of events and when would we finish? That's the best-case scenar-

## The Corporate Prophet

io when you look at it in conjunction with the 'Who?' question."

"Then I ask myself if I have enough funds, what might go wrong and if I've got a 'Plan B'."

He looked around the room, "This questioning doesn't mean you'll take ages even to get started. I get everyone in one room or one call and get things sorted in one go."

"We're really amazed at the speed at which you get your planning through and at the same time keep your delivery solid." Kathy commended. "But before I forget, can you explain little bit on the funding aspect."

"Sure," Ony smiled, "I had almost started worrying whether you were listening to my gibberish at all."

"All plans would need some funding. While all the promised benefits have risks of over-projection, funding is usually under-projected. I first ask questions to get these projections robust. When I'm able to tell myself that I've done a good job on this, I close my eyes and I see a face emerging from nowhere asking me this question—'While your returns are in the future, your expenses are in the present, do you understand?'"

"Yeah, come to the point, I know who you're referring to," Kathy pushed him.

Ony smiled and continued.

"Well that question forces my people to think if we have any ideas to generate 'additional' resources to fund our plan. Can we phase out a brand? Can we stop a product line? Can we cut spending on an existing brand? You know those sorts of questions. Essentially, trying to understand if some resources can be freed. It's only in the end that we come to you."

"Good you do that," Kathy commented, "otherwise; we'd have a debt mountain large enough to crush all of us!"

"Another important part is holding effective meetings with clear agendas, and neat meeting minutes with what, who, and when defined. The agenda is circulated reasonably ahead of time to allow people to prepare and the minutes are circulated shortly after the meeting. In my mind, I'm always going to be open for changes due to genuine reasons but I don't allow for slack due to incompetence. In fact, after so many years of practice, our teams have perfected this art and in any case, we don't have any incompetent people."

"All that you explained before this sounds like project management to me," Hu looked at Ony.

"Call it by any name, 'Execution', 'Project Management' for unique deliverables, or 'Operational Excellence' for routine deliverables", emphasized John, "just get it done!"

"I don't find too many people around who can though," Hu expressed her concern, "how do we make people learn this skill?"

"The foremost is through association with people like Ony", Kris responded.

"I have personally learnt a lot on this from Ony, and, I'm sure all of us have. His team members, of course, have developed tremendously."

"I also believe that we have to recognize and reward achievements in execution that promotes its importance and makes people interested in this."

"Then, of course, you can have well designed programs to train people."

King raised his hand, "do we have people who can design such programs?"

There was a brief burst of laughter at this. That allowed King to rise and step out for the break that he needed.

"That's an important question," Hu started after she had stopped laughing. "And the answer is we don't always need to have all the expertise in-house. We, at least, know where to go to. There are people who specialize in that and have proven records of accomplishment. Also, we know how to interview them and select the right ones for us. We may not always succeed in the first go, but then instead of not doing anything at all, we can always experiment and change as necessary."

"Change, yes, we must," Kris said in a tone that conveyed he looked at change in a positive manner.

## 19. Change

"Do we have an alternative here? Since we are linked with everything else in the world and since everything else is changing continuously, we necessarily undergo change. Even internally, the churn is continuous. So change shall happen."

"We, however, would be leaving things completely to chance if we give up and start behaving like victims of this monster that's beyond our control. Change isn't a monster. It's a concept. Just like 'Time'. The concept of 'Time' doesn't harm or benefit us. The concept of 'Change' doesn't harm or benefit us. How we use these concepts is up to us. There would always be many things beyond our control. Nevertheless, there would be some things that we can influence."

"In fact, we can direct change in many scenarios. Introduction of any new process is change. Modification of any existing process is change. Hiring is change, promotion is change, and separation is change too!"

"Of course, and some separations can be devastating," John commented.

"Some of these would be of high importance and potential impact," Kris generalized and continued.

Mohan Pandey

"Such changes need to be managed carefully, to the extent that is pragmatically possible."

"First of all, you need to imagine how and whom the change is going to impact. All the key stakeholders need to be adequately informed. In fact, you would do well to have their buy-in beforehand."

"Second, you should lay out the process very clearly and transparently. What's expected and when, needs to be charted out."

"Third, ensure that there's a vent in the system. Have controls, but don't etch your plan in stone. There's always a possibility that you'd learn something along the way that might be of enough importance to make you modify your plan."

"I have always believed," King was back, "that instead of asking what happened, one should be at the frontier and make change happen."

"Some of the products that we launched were not really waiting for the markets to evolve, those products actually created new markets. In some areas, we are so far ahead of our competition because we set the agenda for change. I'm not boasting, there are hundreds of companies that are innovative, but we are disruptively so."

"Why just products," John quickly pointed out, "some of our key systems are so unique that B-schools have written case studies about them! The way we've woven our fabric is so unique that no one's been able to replicate it though we have always been sharing them with the world."

"It may sound like we are being complacent," Ony smiled, "but some of our brands are so iconic that copying the product is of little use to competition. Our own make by another name might not sell."

"Friends, I'm feeling more comfortable with my decision now," said Kris.

"We're so well positioned that we have this extremely high risk of becoming complacent and secure, if we aren't already. This is the time, right time, when we need this big change. Or else, our sustainability is at stake."

No one missed the point.

## 20. Sustainability

"Popularly, don't we interpret the word 'sustainability' from the perspective of environment and climate change?" asked Henry.

"Yes, and there's lot of merit in using the same for corporate survival. In the long run, we cannot keep behaving irresponsibly and take the environment for granted. If humanity is at risk, don't even ask the question to any corporation or any industry. It becomes trivial then."

"We should continue to be driven by the scientific evidence and work towards creating regulations that encourages environment protection. Even, otherwise we should have our own internal objectives that help the environment. These should be an integrated part of how we do business. We should also continuously invest in new technologies that offer products with better environment quotient. Keep in mind when we were reducing waste from the system, we were also doing some good to the environment."

"On the contrary, in many cases our pursuit of limitless growth has created many other problems that are taking a substantial amount of our time and energy.

Mohan Pandey

Don't be fooled that the increased level of economic activity thus generated, may add to the apparent economic growth. Going one mile down and then climbing one mile back may appear as if you've done a lot of work, but in the end, you've not moved at all!"

"We're trustees of our shareholder's wealth. Our job is to increase this wealth. Our job is to sustain our enterprise and ensure that we have smooth handovers. We're not to be swayed by the quarterly results but to ensure that we build a solid business for the long run."

"In very much the same way, we are trustees of this beautiful world and we should not leave it any poorer for our children."

"Consume we must, what we must. But then we should not get consumed in the process. More than anything else, we should focus on minimizing the use of non-renewable resources across the value chain, that is, if we cannot eliminate the need altogether."

"Also, we should compensate for the renewable resources that are used in equal measure."

"That's good sense, good science, and also good business."

"It may not be that obvious in the beginning, but a carefully integrated view of sustainability in vision and strategy is a smart business choice."

"We should continuously educate our customers and help them make the right choice in favor of our environment. While we do that, our job would still be to offer them the value for their money and we should utilize emerging tools like carbon trading to achieve that."

"Fortunately, we're living in a time when the world is probably at its highest literacy rate. These are the times when people are more and more aware of the larger issues. These are the times when you can easily communicate your agenda and philosophy to the society at large."

"Let me warn you though, if you're not serious about it, and are just paying lip-service, these are also the times when society is watching your lips on a large screen."

# 21. Society

"Don't you think," Kathy asked, "we need to just focus on doing our work right."

"If everyone in the world did that, then society is taken care of. If one is not doing so, the product and services they offer would be rejected and that organization would perish."

"Do you mean," Ony appeared worried at this thought, "that all is well with the world right now?"

"For sure, we're all trying to maximize individual benefits. However, we don't see that we are becoming any happier."

"That's probably because we don't have enough philanthropy yet," Henry observed.

"People who make a lot of money should use their wealth for the improvement of the society in general and the poor in particular. I see a great deal of this has happened in the last century, but may be, it should happen more."

"Giving is good," Kris reflected, "no one's going to carry even a needle to the next world."

"I'm all for philanthropy. However, we need to get our frame right. Are we saying that we should get rich by whatever means and then use the money to do good? Are we sure that we would be in a position to clear our sins in the first place? Overall, would the net be positive? Even if so, isn't some of the harm irreparable?

Getting rich and giving back is good, but is not good enough. You need to look at the means."

"All of us collectively form the society. It's not an alien object that we transact with. What we do for society is also, in a way, what we do for ourselves."

"Imagine a world where we have wealth concentrated in the hands of a few individuals. They would need armies to protect themselves, if at all they can. Even if it were not a complete breakdown of society, you would face continuous struggle and tremendous risks in the system. You would have weak markets and low trust. That kind of environment would erode wealth."

"That's why we have laws written down. They assert our rights. Even if not explicitly defined, our rights are contingent on our duties. As good citizens, our responsibility is not to merely run a social responsibility program; it's our obligation to conduct our business in a socially responsible manner."

"I'm opposed to forcing my personal norms on others. I'm opposed to getting norms forced on me as well. At the same time, I'm aware that if we don't have social norms, all of us will perish. Try driving without any traffic rules!

## The Corporate Prophet

"There would be many opportunities of creating wealth for ourselves and maximizing return for shareholders by indulging in illegal businesses. But then, friends, you should also ask how many of your shareholders would like to share the prison with you. While I say that, let me be very clear, it's not only about being legal, it's about being right. It's about being able to stand in front of your conscience and argue your case."

"In a blind pursuit of short-term growth, you might be borrowing too much from the future. Are you not taking away the share of the generations not yet born? And in any case are you not in danger of inflation engulfing you faster if your borrowing from future is at an unsustainable rate? Economics is an important dimension of human society; however, it's just one dimension. Disastrous when misused, or even when ignored, used wisely, it serves the pursuit of the 'Good' through optimal utilization of resources. Along with that, don't forget the pursuit of 'Truth' and of 'Beauty'."

"Maximize your moral wealth and then give back."

## 22. Ethics

"Aren't moral values and ethics contextual?" Hu asked. "I mean different people and indeed different societies view things differently. Some societies put Individual over Society and some put Society over Individual. Some societies compete with Nature and yet others emphasize on co-existing with Nature."

"I understand what you're saying, Hu," Kris paused and responded.

"There are a couple of key things we need to put in perspective. One is the current global reality where slowly but steadily we're moving close towards the dream of creating a global village. Despite the richness of diversity that we have in our traditions—and which we must maintain—we now have important global forums to discuss and agree on common denominators. Never before in the history of humanity have we been able to have an exchange of ideas at this pace or scale."

"The other is the fact that there are some common principles which all can agree to—do not lie, do not steal, do not kill. Seers and visionaries of the past have articulated similar thoughts in different words—live and let live. We rely on individuals to hold themselves to these standards that epitomize the evolution of human thought. We expect that everyone would exhibit the right behavior even when no one's watching you."

"In the case of a corporation, like us, we cannot leave ethics to chance though. In a global organization, it becomes imperative that there are common rules for everyone. As equal opportunity employers, you'd have people in your organization from a variety of backgrounds. Indeed, you would actively promote diversity. It's extremely critical then, that everyone follows a set of standards that will help the organization work cohesively."

"Of course, none of the organizational standards should be at loggerheads with sovereign constitutions. They do not need to be either."

"Ethics, friends, is one factor so critical that we have a completely independent organization reporting to the board to ensure we all follow the standards. There's no margin for error here."

"Any employee on any day is free to approach this organization, even anonymously, without fear of reprisal if she or he isn't comfortable with any practice or incident observed in the organization that's not in line with the standards of ethics."

"The standards are clearly articulated and translated into all major languages and made available to all employees. And thanks to Henry, we have ensured that we have documented that all employees understand these standards."

"If in doubt, ask. That's about it. Don't assume things here. I repeat, 'no margin of error'.

"The repercussions are clear as well. The board doesn't tolerate deviations here. Thorough enquiries would be conducted and the organization reserves its rights to act to preserve its integrity."

"Hu has already done an excellent job of creating stories around these values and these are infused across the organization systematically. She was right in pointing out to me that we remember stories more than standard texts."

"Maintaining the integrity of the organization is the most important job of the leaders of the organization. That's what differentiates leaders from the great leaders."

## 23. Leadership

"It may sound like a stupid question, but, what's your view on that age old question—whether leaders are born or made." Ony again.

"You could argue both ways and mount evidence in support of your argument. For me, it's a matter of belief. Take the myth and mystic away from the word 'leader'. To lead is to take ownership and accountability. To lead is to build trust. To lead is to be able to deal with complexity and chaos with courage and vision. To lead is to be able to take decisions. And, to lead is to serve."

"I believe in the infinite potential of human beings. I believe that it's for us to unlock that potential. Great leaders, in fact, help others unlock this potential. We become leaders when we stand up for something."

"We see many people around with a natural leadership demonstrated since childhood and we do see many people around who trained themselves and worked hard on it and were eventually able to lead millions."

"What I have learnt, though, is this. Even if it's in you, even if you're a natural, you are but an uncut diamond. You have to go through the grind. It's great

Mohan Pandey

if you find a mentor to coach you through, otherwise be observant and learn from your experience. May the lessons from the masters be your guide when you embark on this path."

"It doesn't matter, what the answer to that question is. Nevertheless, if the answer were that it's in your genes, I'd tend to think, that wouldn't be a very useful answer. So take this as the answer, 'you can develop yourself as a leader'. Wherever you are, whatever the scope of your work is, the day you decide to lead, you start on this magnificent journey of leadership."

"As leaders of organizations we need to be able to effectively communicate. Leaders link their organization to the external world. Keeping their organizations relevant to the emerging global environment is important. It's also important to effectively engage with the key stakeholders."

"Many a times, the most complicated messages, internally or externally, can be conveyed through stories. Leaders would not only know how get the story right, they would also be good at delivering those stories."

"Leading an organization essentially means leading the people in the organization. Leaders therefore must have legitimacy and they must develop trust."

"They consistently demonstrate the highest standards of behavior. They become role models that parents would like their children to emulate. Moreover, when they commit any mistake, which for sure they would sometimes as all human beings are fallible, they would own up."

"Leaders would themselves plant fruits trees which would be enjoyed by the future generations; and, they would inspire others to do likewise."

"Leaders would achieve true success on the criteria of The Truth, The Good, and The Beauty; of course, that would also add value to their enterprises. They would inspire others to do likewise."

"Of course, while doing all this, they would know that they were trustees of a larger purpose, and therefore, they would be humble."

"Leaders would, if I may paraphrase the words of wisdom of seers from the yore, 'rise, awaken and stop not till the vision is realized'."

## 24. Evening: The Dinner

Kris invited the team home for dinner that evening. As always, Maya welcomed everyone, but they noticed something was amiss.

During dinner, Kris mentioned that he had been diagnosed with a rare disease and that it would be a miracle if he lived beyond a couple of months. He reiterated that he would spend the rest of his time working for underprivileged children. He had been using his vacations for a long time to volunteer and donate for this cause. Now he wanted to do this full time. He believed he already had some ideas that could revolutionize this area.

He appeared exhausted as he asked Maya to read out the brief note he had written.

"On my way back from work today, I reflected on the meeting we had. More than what you learnt from me, I guess, I learnt today from you. It became clear to me that while I had not engaged in any separate spiritual pursuit, I had always had attempted to follow the Triad, even without realizing it. The Truth, the Good, and the Beauty. My accelerated career was a by-product of that pursuit. My attempts to find how

Mohan Pandey

our actions link with the Triad necessarily resulted in Systems Thinking, which then brought Sustainability and Society to the forefront of my objectives. Once that was in place, the only way I could work was through optimization and continuous improvement. As much as the organization improved, I also improved myself. Thoughts of my retirement day, always kept me down to earth and I was able to shed my ego. I was doing what I liked doing. I ensured that our organization had all the organs that were needed and that they remained healthy. I didn't short change future for the present and balanced current investment needs with those for innovation. I trusted people and people delivered. That put us on a virtuous cycle. We shared both our successes and failures, both our upsides and risks, with the external world and established trust there as well. Also, I never took anything away from my family's share for my career's sake. I can feel the love and affection Maya and Abni blessed me with all the time. Now it all makes sense. You don't have to do anything complicated. Do something meaningful and do it in the right manner. And, however, exhausted you feel at the end of the day, do take time to look at the beautiful moon, whenever it comes out to shower its love on you."

He looked outside; it indeed was a beautiful full moon. Maya's gaze was fixed on his calm face.

## The Corporate Prophet

She shared with the group that Kris was thankful to God that he was able to discharge his duties in office without any problem so far. Abni, their son, was to be home the next day as his vacation was to start. He would be with them when the press release goes public.

It was a silent night after that.

The next quarterly results for the company again beat the Street. The company launched its next breakthrough product, a month ahead of schedule under John's leadership, who was elevated to the CEO position. Ony had moved to the COO role and had promoted Jane to Marketing Head. Nobel Prizes were to be announced soon and King was a favorite if online polls were any indication. He was the next one in the great tradition of Langmuir who was the first from any industrial research lab to win a Nobel.

The team was planning to publish a book based on their notes from that last meeting because they believed that millions across the world could benefit from that knowledge. They had dispatched the first draft for Maya's review today. It was to be named 'The Corporate Prophet'.

# About The Author

Mohan Pandey leads Operations and Project Management for an immensely productive R&D site for a global biopharmaceutical company. He has successfully delivered on highly complex, large-scale strategic projects in his over twelve years of experience.

He is a scientist by training and is passionate about innovation, learning and mentoring. He has guided students from prestigious business schools and continues to encourage entrepreneurs through MentorEdge.

An alumnus of the Indian Institute of Management, Ahmedabad and of the Jadavpur University, Calcutta, he is a member of the American Finance Association, and is certified by the Project Management Institute, Pennsylvania. He has several national and international papers and presentations to his credit. He takes strong interest in literature and writes short stories and poetry.

contact@mohanpandey.in
www.mohanpandey.in

www.ingramcontent.com/pod-product-compliance
Lightning Source LLC
Chambersburg PA
CBHW030752180526
45163CB00003B/988